P9-CKU-723

ALSO BY JENNIE NASH

Altared States

The
Victoria's Secret Catalog
Never Stops Coming

*And Other Lessons I Learned
from Breast Cancer*

Jennie Nash

SCRIBNER

New York London Toronto Sydney Singapore

SCRIBNER
1230 Avenue of the Americas
New York, NY 10020

For information about special discounts for bulk purchases,
please contact Simon & Schuster Special Sales:
1-800-465-6798 or business@simonandschuster.com

Designed by Kyoko Watanabe
Text set in Berling

Manufactured in the United States of America

1 3 5 7 9 10 8 6 4 2

Library of Congress Cataloging-in-Publication Data
Nash, Jennie.
The Victoria's Secret catalog never stops coming : and other lessons I learned from
breast cancer / Jennie Nash.
p. cm.
1. Nash, Jennie—Health. 2. Breast—Cancer—Patients—United States—Biography.
I. Title.
RC280.B8 N375 2001
362.1'9699449'0092—dc21
[B]   2001034173
ISBN 0-7432-1979-1

Page 141: Excerpt from Maya Angelou's *Wouldn't Take Nothing for My Journey Now,*
"In All Ways a Woman," published by Random House.

For Carlyn and Emily,
in memory of
Lisa Capps
and
Lori Molina

I am a frayed and nibbled survivor in a fallen world and I am getting along. I am aging and eaten and have done my share of eating, too. I am not washed and beautiful, in control of a shining world in which everything fits, but instead am wandering awed about on a splintered wreck I've come to care for, whose gnawed trees breathe a delicate air, whose bloodied and scarred creatures are my dearest companions, and whose beauty beats and shines not in its imperfections, but overwhelmingly in spite of them, under the wind-rent clouds, upstream and down.

—Annie Dillard, *Pilgrim at Tinker Creek*

Contents

Contents

The Victoria's Secret Catalog
Never Stops Coming

Introduction

Most of us can't do much to find a cure for breast cancer. We can write a check or take a fund-raising walk, but we're not the ones in the lab working with vaccines and genes or coming up with new theories of detection that might make the mammogram seem archaic. What we can do—whether we're looking back on a cancer experience, helping someone else through a cancer experience, or living through the horror right this minute—is tell our story. Stories help. Stories heal. Your story might be the very thing that saves someone's life or helps them get through the night. It might be the only thing that brings you a measure of peace.

It's not always an easy or natural thing to tell your own story. Two days after I was diagnosed with cancer, a good friend of mine—another writer—wrote me a brief e-mail: "You *are* taking notes, aren't you?" I cracked up, because it was so preposterous an idea. During the many sleepless nights I had during my illness, however, this story started to come alive in my head. While my husband and our two little girls slept soundly in the quiet of our dark house, I began to write it down. I wrote about how my instincts are really good, my kids are really resilient, my dad will fold my underwear, and how sometimes the only difference between getting to live and having to die is luck. I wrote a series of lessons. I wrote about things I had learned and ways I had changed, and I realized that I got wise having breast cancer. I'm a wise old lady at the age of thirty-six. If you have survived this disease or helped someone survive it or helped someone leave this world because of it, you're probably wise, too. You have a story to tell and I think you should tell it, whether it's written on paper, whispered ear to ear, or shouted out on a fund-raising walk. It may not be a cure, but it's a truth, and it can make a difference.

Survival Is a Matter of Instinct

You know your body better than anyone else. If you think you have cancer or you dream you have cancer or you have a nagging, persistent belief that the cancer you conquered has recurred, then keep pushing for answers until you're sure, one way or the other. Even if you have a long history of being a hysterical hypochondriac, trust your instincts. Finding cancer early saves lives, and it's just about the only really sure thing that does.

I imagined I had cancer before I knew I had it. The idea of it crept into my consciousness like a song that I couldn't stop singing—a melody I couldn't remember ever learning, but whose particular sound was stuck in my head all the same, insisting on being heard.

The first faint notes came from a local news report in

my hometown of Santa Barbara, California, and though I now live a hundred miles to the south, the flurry of phone calls that followed—"Did you hear?" "Have you talked to her?"—obliterated the barriers of distance: Lisa, a dear friend from high school, had been diagnosed with advanced metastatic lung cancer. This was news in that town because Lisa was the daughter of the city's congresswoman who had won her husband's seat after his sudden, midterm death from a heart attack two years before. It was both awful and amazing, like learning that lightning had struck in the same place twice. I immediately picked up the phone and called Lisa, hoping that the reports were wrong, hoping that it was a terrible rumor, hoping—uncharitably—that maybe they'd gotten the name wrong and it was Lisa's little sister or brother who was ill.

Nathan, Lisa's husband, answered the phone—and I pictured him stationed there in the living room of their Berkeley home, stoic and generous, rising to the occasion of a phone ringing off the hook. I didn't know Nathan well, but I recalled how he had pursued Lisa in college, convinced that she was the woman he was destined to marry, and how Lisa had hemmed and hawed, concerned with the philosophical questions of how you could decide on one person to share your life, and how you could know when you'd found him. It seemed a laughable debate, when Lisa finally brought Nathan home: she was a very tall, very blond, very blue-eyed woman with a happy, open face, and Nathan looked like a carbon copy who had been designed for the express purpose of being her life's mate.

He told me the same thing he told all the other stunned callers who dialed their house in Berkeley that night: "It's true. We just found out. She'll call when we know more."

⌘

At Santa Barbara High School in the mid-1980s, Lisa was a homecoming princess, a nationally competitive long-distance swimmer, valedictorian of our class, my neighbor, and the first person I had ever met who recognized, understood, applauded, and shared my ambitious nature. She was a smart girl who prided herself on her smartness and for that alone I would have loved her because it gave me the confidence to feel proud, too. We took the exact same schedule of advanced placement courses and pushed and prodded each other to achieve the grand ambitions we both nurtured like pearls. At the time, we weren't sure exactly what those ambitions were or where they might take us; we only felt the fierceness of the desire to do something or be someone, and that desire brought us together—sometimes in unexpected ways and places.

The summer after our junior year, I went to England for an immersion course in Shakespeare's plays. I was thrilled about the adventure but homesick from the moment I stepped on the plane in Los Angeles. I was the youngest student on the trip by five years—the only high school student—and I not only felt scared of the intellectual challenge, I felt scared of the reality of being in a foreign country with a group of strangers. We had two days in London before going out to Stratford, where we would be studying. On one of those days, we went to visit St. Paul's Cathedral. I was sitting in one of the pews, staring up at the dome and listening to the hushed sounds of a throng of people trying to be silent, when I heard someone say my name—too loudly. I snapped around to see Lisa, standing there in the aisle, towering above the crowd.

I sprang up to hug her. "What are you doing here?" I demanded, thinking she had somehow come to give me a message or bring me something I'd forgotten to pack.

"My dad just decided to come," she explained. I looked over her shoulder at her dad, as if his presence would confirm the fact of her being there.

"But how did you know I would be here?" I pressed, thinking that somehow my mother—a travel agent—had passed along some inside information.

"I had no idea you'd be here," Lisa explained, laughing. "I pictured you watching *A Winter's Tale* in some dark old theater in Stratford."

"That's Wednesday," I said, feeling excited again about doing what I'd come to England to do.

During the winter months of our last year in high school, Lisa and I would race off campus at lunchtime in her red convertible VW Bug to search our mailboxes for college acceptance letters. Lisa got more than I did, but we both eventually settled on colleges we were sure would help us shape and launch our dreams. She ended up at Stanford and I went east to Wellesley, three thousand miles away.

After college, we each married and we each had two children—boys for Lisa, girls for me. We lived near each other for short periods of time in New York and then in Los Angeles, but our friendship didn't become a relationship about our kids and husbands. It remained a private encouragement society. Lisa encouraged me to keep writing what I wanted to write rather than what other people wanted me to write, and I encouraged her to stay true to herself and her own ideas as she made her way through the maze of academia. She was working toward a degree in narrative psychology and quietly doing innovative and award-winning work that brought together elements of linguistics and psychology. She was interested in the way that people with various mental disorders tell stories about themselves, why they tell them, and what they mean.

During her third winter as an assistant professor of psychology at Berkeley, Lisa caught a cough that wouldn't go away. Instead of being told she had strep throat or bronchitis or pneumonia like so many other people going into the cold season, she was told she had lung cancer and that it had already invaded the bones in her spine. No one ever talked about how long she had to live, or even whether she would live, but no one had to.

Metastatic lung cancer, even in an otherwise healthy thirty-five-year-old woman, is a staggeringly virulent disease.

I wanted to fly to Berkeley immediately to do something to help—but everyone wanted to fly to Berkeley to do something to help and there wasn't room for us all, either at the house or in Lisa's illness. Lisa's mom would be there as Lisa started her chemo, her sister would follow, and Lisa and Nathan had a network of devoted and generous friends who knew their two boys, knew the routines of their days, and knew what was needed to help. "Don't come," Lisa said. "It's too overwhelming right now." I was just an out-of-town high school friend who wasn't needed at the center of the crisis. I felt helpless and stung, and I did the only things I felt I could: I worried; I talked constantly with everyone I knew who knew her; I mailed her cards and letters, quotes, and stories; and I bought her a hat.

Lisa expected to lose her hair immediately from the chemo and she'd decided not to wear a wig. She'd gone out with her mother to look at them but couldn't bring herself to buy one or wear one. I imagined I would have done the same. I scoured the stores for hats that looked soft and wearable, and found a cotton hat in a watery blue batik print that looked exactly like the kind of thing Lisa would wear. Blue, to match her eyes. Bright, to match her spirit. Not too fussy or prissy. I felt pleased with myself as I wrapped the hat in tissue paper and sealed it in a padded envelope, but as soon as I mailed the package, I realized how small my efforts were. They didn't do anything meaningful to help Lisa heal, and they didn't do anything to alleviate my fear for my friend.

I bolted awake in the middle of the night with my brain spinning, imagining what it must be like to have lung cancer. I pictured Lisa's breath moving slowly in and out of her lungs as she lay awake at night picturing the mutant cells that wouldn't accept the message to stop reproducing. I could hear David, her five-year-old son, coming up to her and saying something innocent—"I can get you a Band-Aid for your cancer, Mom"—and the tears that would spring to her eyes as she had to either lie and thank him or tell the truth and shatter him. I pictured her husband looking at her with an expression that couldn't possibly hide how scared he was that she would die and leave him alone with a house, two boys, and a life that was meant to be shared.

I got so good at imagining the dread of the disease that after only a few nights I decided that it must not be my imagination at all. I decided that I, too, must have cancer. I'd had a small tightness in a vague place on the left side of my chest, and for months I'd thought of it as a pulled muscle or mild recurrent heartburn. I was now convinced that it was a mass of insatiable cancer cells marching through my breast.

Cancer works well as an imagined illness because it generally has no discernible cause. Unless you work in an asbestos plant or smoke two packs of cigarettes a day, you can't ever really say why cancer turns up in your body. It could be the hormones in the milk, the pesticides on the fruit, the smog in the air, the stress in our lives, or that nitrate-filled bologna sandwich you had for lunch every single day from kindergarten through sixth grade. It might have to do with how early you got your period, how late you had your children, how little you nursed them, how much you depended on birth control pills—or all of the above. Anyone could get cancer, for any of those reasons or for none of them, so why not me? What if me?

I'm not a hypochondriac in the usual sense of the word. I don't imagine myself *actually* plagued with horrible disease, complete with real or even imaginary symptoms. I come, in fact, from unusually healthy stock: in my family, no one gets sick and they live so long, they don't so much die as wither and decay. My feared diseases are always hypothetical, things that might happen sometime out there in the void of the future. They're the mental exercises of someone who's read hundreds of books about things that fall apart, of someone who was a child of divorce and learned early that nothing stays whole forever. Other than visits related to pregnancy and childbirth, I'd been to the doctor exactly three times in the last ten years.

Still, as I stepped into my family practitioner's office, I was aware that my story sounded paranoid: I had a sore spot on my breast that got more pronounced when my friend found out she had lung cancer and I realized there was nothing I could do to help. I put on the paper gown, sat on the table, and entertained thoughts of slipping back into my clothes and sneaking out the door. The only thing that kept me in place was a poster on the wall next to the examining table. It was an illustration of the lungs, showing one red healthy lung and one gray cancerous lung. It was a detailed, four-color blowup of Lisa's exact disease.

When the doctor showed up with my chart in her hand and asked what the trouble was, I explained about the sore spot and quickly added that there was also this thing about my friend who was just my age, with two kids just like mine, who'd gone in with a cough and come out with cancer. My doctor listened, nodded, and did a breast exam. "There's nothing here," she said, creasing her forehead and shaking her head. "I think it's just a sore rib, but to make yourself feel better, why don't you go get a mammogram?"

I could have gone home and forgotten about it, convinced that I'd followed my paranoia to its furthest practical end. Most women don't get their first mammogram until they're forty. Many HMOs would prefer that we not get into the habit until we're fifty, when our breasts aren't as dense and our odds of getting a clean bill of health aren't as good. But Lisa had already proven to me that cancer knows no age limits, and I was eager to clean the slate of my imagination. A week later I stood half naked in a cold room and had a technician with cold hands squeeze my breasts between the cold plates of a cold machine and tell me not to breathe. She stepped behind a shield, produced a sound similar to the one made by Darth Vader's light saber, then told me to tie up my gown and wait while she showed my films to the radiologist.

I waited in the examining room, thinking of Lisa. She had sat in a room just like this, waiting to hear the results of a test just like mine, and someone had walked in and said the word *cancer.* What would it be like to hear news like that? How had she felt? How would *I* feel? I decided that it would be easy to be shocked but hard to be surprised; after all, I was sitting in a medical facility whose entire purpose for being was to find cancer in women's breasts. It wasn't as if they were going to come back and tell me there was something wrong with my big toe. They were either going to find cancer or they weren't. I was either going to continue to be a witness to my friend's struggle to live—a worried outsider with my nose pressed against the glass—or I was going to join her struggle in the most personal and perilous way possible. I thought these thoughts, but I didn't for one second believe that anyone was actually going to walk back into the room and announce that there was something wrong.

When the radiologist came back, she confirmed what my doctor had determined: that there was nothing but healthy breast tissue in the place I was complaining about. I nodded, easily convinced. She went on to point out, however, that there were tiny calcifications in my *other* breast that she wanted to keep an eye on. "Lots of women have them," she explained, as if we were talking about oily skin or cellulite, "and ninety percent of the time they don't mean a thing, especially in someone your age. Come back in six months and we'll check them again."

Sure, no problem, we'll check them again, I thought. As far as I was concerned, what I had feared had not occurred. I hadn't imagined anything wrong anywhere else in my body besides my left breast, and since there was nothing there, I relaxed the grip of my imagination. No more dreams of disease woke me in the middle of the night.

∽

For the next six months, Lisa continued to battle cancer. She didn't like to talk about her treatments or their side effects or her future; whenever we talked, she always wanted to know how *my* kids were doing or how *my* work was going, so I told self-conscious anecdotes about Emily's swimming lessons, Carlyn's spelling tests, and the mysterious error messages I was getting from my hard drive. I pieced together the story of her illness from conversations with friends in New York, San Francisco, Washington, and Santa Barbara. We pooled our knowledge—she told me this, she told me that, so-and-so's mother ran into Lisa's mother who said such-and-such about her prognosis. Lisa's cancer was inoperable. She had two courses of high-dose chemotherapy to try to halt the tumor in her lungs and spine. She used yoga, meditation, visualization, and acupuncture to try to turn the considerable power of her brain against her disease.

Although I continued to offer and to ask, Lisa still didn't want me to make the short trip from L.A. to

Berkeley to visit her because she was never sure which days were going to be good and which days were going to be bad. I didn't care about being there on a bad day, but that was because I wanted to visit for my *own* comfort— not hers. It was maddening to have to respect her wishes and stay in L.A. I wanted to be near her, to do something to help her, to see with my own eyes the truth of what she was going through. Instead, I continued to send her cards—quotes from Annie Dillard's *Pilgrim at Tinker Creek* and drafts of a story I was writing about my irrational desire for Carlyn to love playing the piano even though I never had. She'd write me back when she was able to—cheerful e-mail messages and quick notes in her distinctive, loopy scrawl:

> *I LOVE the Annie Dillard quote. I couldn't make it through the book on my first try, but now I'm inspired. I DO remember when we went to hear her speak in New York. I remember being pleased about something she said about God. I'm hanging in there. I go back to Stanford for more chemo tomorrow, which I'm trying hard not to dread. I think I feel the positive effects already.*
>
> *Love, Lisa*
>
> *P.S. Did I thank you for the hat? I LOVE it. It fits perfectly and it's a great color and it's comfortable . . . and I am bald.*

I posted Lisa's cards on the bulletin board in my office like prayer flags and continued to feel that there must be something more I could do.

∽

When I got a reminder letter from my radiologist that it was time for the six-month follow-up, I grudgingly made the appointment, showed up at the doctor's office, and went through the whole cold-fingered routine one more time. After the mammogram, the technician said the same thing she'd said before—to tie up my gown and wait until she showed the film to the radiologist—but this time she came back and said she was going to do a magnification view, just to make sure they got the picture they wanted. Good idea, I thought. I stood in front of the machine again, held my breath, then sat down and flipped through *House Beautiful* while I waited. The technician came back a second time and announced that the doctor wanted to do an ultrasound in the room at the end of the hall. It began to register that something unusual was going on. Why did they want to do an ultrasound? Hadn't the radiologist said that 90 percent of women have these calcifications that turned out to be nothing? I asked the technician what was going on, but all she was allowed to say was that the doctor would answer my questions.

The doctor—the radiologist—soon came into the ultrasound room and spread a cold gel on my breast with cold hands. "What are you looking at?" I squeaked.

"It looks like the shape of these calcifications has changed," she told me. "I want to confirm it." This didn't sound so bad, but then she went on: "Calcifications that are naturally occurring are shaped like teacups. They don't change. Calcifications that come from tumors have a different shape."

I stared at the ceiling. Tumors?

She started to work the machine, peering at the black-and-white image on the little screen. After only a few seconds, she said, "We're definitely looking at a biopsy here."

"A biopsy?" I said. For a millisecond I wondered if she was joking.

"We do it right in the office," she explained. "It's a simple procedure. Doesn't hurt a bit." She handed me a brochure that was supposed to answer all my questions and I took it, even though I couldn't think of a thing to ask.

∽

I was in such complete denial that cancer could be found that I spent the next week planning for Carlyn's birthday party and preparing material for a writers' workshop I was scheduled to attend the following weekend. When I thought about the upcoming biopsy, I thought only about the procedure itself. I was scheduled to have what's called a stereotactic core biopsy. I looked up the term on the Web and learned that it was a relatively new procedure, which allows the doctor to pinpoint tissue on a computerized image of the breast and take a core sample all the way around it. It reminded me of a geology class I took in college. When a friend told me that a friend of hers had recently had a core biopsy and that it had hurt, I called the radiologist and asked her questions about anesthesia and whether she thought there was any problem with my driving to the writers' workshop after the biopsy was over. I never even formulated the question "What if . . . ?" When my mother insisted on driving two hours to be with me for the biopsy on Friday, I thought it was unnecessary and arbitrary. I wondered why she suddenly felt so maternal.

I was enormously grateful, in the end, that my mother had had the foresight to make the trip because the biopsy did, in fact, hurt—a *lot*—and it was a comfort to know someone was sitting in the waiting room waiting for me.

First, the radiologist made me lie down on a rigid, wavy table, then made me place my breast in a cutout where she could reach it. Once I was in position, she told me not to move. She gave me a local anesthetic in my breast that was supposed to halt the pain the way Novocain does at the dentist's. It didn't. She tried five separate times to numb my breast, but it never completely worked. "You're setting the record for anesthesia," she cheerfully explained. Each time she turned the needle to get a sample of more tissue, I felt as if someone was plunging a knife into the soft underbelly of my body and spinning it in circles. I sobbed, recalling—too late—my body's unwillingness to respond to the best medications on the maternity floor and feeling sorry for myself to be in this position yet again. The nurse brought me a Kleenex and reminded me not to move. When the forty-five-minute biopsy procedure was over, I sat up on the table, held a cotton ball over the pencil-size hole in my breast, and wept—both because it was over and because it had hurt so badly. The radiologist felt so sorry for me, she allowed my mother to come back and sit with me in the patients' waiting area while I held an ice pack to my breast.

I spent the next few days at the writers' workshop and, though my chest was wrapped up like a mummy's, I got so involved in the people and the work that I was able to keep any thoughts of results at bay. On Monday, however, I hung around the house all day waiting to hear from the doctor, and by the time the kids got home from school, I couldn't stand it anymore. I figured my fate was already sealed. It was either going to be cancer or it wasn't and I couldn't do a thing to change it.

"Let's go to the pumpkin patch," I said, and began to round up shoes and jackets. I hated the pumpkin patch. It was an old corner car wash that had been turned into a dirty, money-grubbing petting zoo–amusement park–pumpkin patch and would, a few weeks later, be turned into a dirty, money-grubbing Santa's lap–amusement park–Christmas tree lot, and it smelled of sadness and ruin to me. It was a good place to wait for news that had a 50 percent chance of causing sadness and ruin. I called to invite one of Carlyn's friends from down the street because Carlyn begged me to and I didn't have the will to resist. We piled in the car and went to pick out picked-over pumpkins.

The call came while we were gone. It was a vague and foreboding message from my family practitioner: "I need to see you tomorrow. Call my secretary and make an appointment." While the kids drew faces on their pumpkins with permanent markers they usually aren't allowed to touch, I dialed the doctor's number, desperate to catch her before she left for the day. I shook from the inside out—my heart and my stomach fluttering while my fingers steadily dialed. My doctor came to the phone almost instantly and told me that I did, in fact, have breast cancer. It was an early, as-yet-unfeelable cancer snaking through the milk ducts in my right breast, where my imagination had never strayed.

I called Rob at work and uttered three words: "I have cancer."

I put the emphasis on the word *cancer*, with a slight questioning intonation, as if I was calling to say that I had some rare disease that you only get from horned purple ticks deep in the Amazon rain forest and I wondered how such a thing had possibly come to pass. He uttered four words back in a flat and stunned tone: "I'll be right home."

I immediately dialed the radiologist's office, praying she was still there. She came instantly to the phone, but her voice was far less comforting than my family doctor's had been. She spoke in a cool and competent voice that was just the tiniest bit rushed. She explained that my cancer had yet to invade beyond the breast, but described the cell type as being aggressive. When I asked her what I should do next, she told me I would have to find an oncologist and a surgeon. Hearing those words—*oncologist, surgeon*—was more of a jolt than hearing the word *cancer.*

Rob arrived home in the middle of this phone call, dropped his briefcase in the front hallway, walked directly back to where I was still talking on the phone, and kneeled next to my chair. It wasn't until I saw him that I started to cry. I covered my face with my hands and sobbed. I hated that he had to be part of this. His mother had died of breast cancer only six years before and he didn't deserve to have to face it all over again. He didn't deserve anything besides a healthy wife, and I was now and forever after going to be someone who was at risk of forcing him to make good on his promise to love in sickness as well as in health. That wasn't the picture I had painted for our life together. I had always envisioned Rob being the one to die first.

When they heard me crying, the girls came running. "Don't worry," I said, waving them back to their pumpkins, "I just got some bad news from the doctor."

"Do you have to get a shot?" Emily asked.

"Something like that," I lied.

✑

I felt fragile, as if moving too quickly or too suddenly would cause the cancer to spread through my body like wildfire. I felt physically diminished, as if my body displaced less air than it had only a few moments before. But I also felt immensely alert, as if I'd stepped out from the darkness into the clear light of day. I hadn't been able to see my cancer and I hadn't been able to feel it, but I had heard it calling. There was pride in that, and there was power, and I knew exactly what I had to do: get it out of my body.

Lesson #2

Bad News Does Less Damage When It's Shared

There's nothing more liberating than talking about your disease. It tends to instantly get you support, understanding, sympathy, camaraderie—and even advice about where to buy comfortable bras. It disarms the cancer from being something secret or sacred and puts the power into your hands. You can pick up the phone, send a fax, write an e-mail, knock on a neighbor's door—anything that helps you tell your story and send it out into the world of people who love and care about you.

Having cancer was, at first, more of an amazement than anything else. Far from feeling as if I'd been diagnosed with a disease that could be fatal, I felt as if Lisa—and my imagination—had saved my life. I felt lucky that the cancer was discovered so early. I recalled the story a colleague of mine had told about the day her short movie was nominated for an Academy Award and how everyone she'd ever known had called to say congratulations. Her news was so awesome, it brought people out of the woodwork to register their amazement. My news felt equally intense. The odds of such a thing happening—of finding an unfeelable cancer through an unscheduled mammogram—were about as good as winning an Oscar. It was terrible, but in a perverse way it was exhilarating. I wanted to tell everyone I knew.

This instinct—to tell—was not new for me. I've never been a very good keeper of secrets. By talking and writing about my dissatisfactions, disappointments, and desires, I can face them, shape them, and understand them. I have the illusion, anyway, of being in control. Added to this penchant for telling is the fact that I don't like things looming over me. I like getting things over with. I like resolution. The worst thing I could imagine, in those first few hours of knowing I had cancer, was knowing that there were people who loved me who didn't yet know my news.

As soon as I stopped crying, I repeated to Rob all the frightening words I'd just heard. He held me and then went to make the girls hot dogs. Thrilled at the unexpected windfall of dinner in front of the TV, they plopped down to watch a movie about a witch who learns to trust her powers.

I called my mom first. Her phone rang once, twice,

three times. As her answering machine kicked in, I made a split-second decision to leave a message: "This is me. I have cancer. I don't know anything else, but I see the doctor tomorrow. Call when you get a chance." I wasn't thinking about how cruel it would be for her to press the button on her machine, expecting messages about a client's trip to Pakistan or Peru, about board meetings and breakfast dates, and hear instead that her daughter had been diagnosed with breast cancer. I was just doing what I felt driven to do.

After leaving that first message, I started dialing wildly—my sister, my dad, my college roommate, my next-door neighbor, my dear friend Lori. Not one single person was home. I had just heard that I had cancer and everyone was at the grocery store or the gym or on the road home from work. Why weren't they instantly and totally available to hear my news? I blurted out the fact of my cancer on message machines all across the country. It was more important for me to tell than to engage in any kind of a dialogue. I wanted the news out of me, where it felt like it would do less harm.

Within a few minutes, people started to call back. Everyone was shocked by my news, even the ones who knew I was going in for a biopsy, and their responses were dramatic and sympathetic. They gasped. They cried. I was thirty-five years old, the mother of two small girls, and I had cancer. It was horrible! It was shocking! It was amazing that it was found!

By the next morning, my cancer had become a story

that I could retell, reduce, and rebroadcast with a prescribed emotion. It was no longer new and raw. The
transformation came when I was sitting at my desk pre-
tending I was working, when what I was really doing was
waiting to go to the doctor's for proof that I really did
have cancer. I still held out hope that what she had told
me hadn't been true—that I had misheard her or misin-
terpreted the implications or that, perhaps, she had
called the wrong patient. I imagined having to call everyone back and say I'm sorry, I got it wrong; I'm fine.

In the middle of this bout of denial, Doug, another
old high school friend who had helped me piece together
the reality of Lisa's illness, happened to see that I was on-
line and zapped me a chatty little message. I hit the reply
button and wrote a brief, blasé account of my diagnosis.
He replied to my reply by calling on the phone and saying, *"What?"*

I launched into the story one more time. My favorite
part was the part about its being a miracle that it was
found. I liked telling that part because I didn't want my
friends and family to feel wholly sad. I wasn't looking for
pity; there was too much responsibility in that. I liked the
miracle part because it exactly captured the way I felt:
shocked that I had cancer and blessed that I knew it so
early.

During the flurry of phone calls that first night and
day, I wasn't the only one in the house to answer the
phone. I wasn't the only one to tell my story. Rob sometimes picked up the phone and told his version of the

news we'd just received. At first, as I listened, I would edit his remarks in my head, thinking, Don't forget to add this or That's not exactly true! Sometimes I simply thought, Give me the phone. I didn't want Rob telling my sister how I felt, just as I didn't want my friend Denise running into my friend Nancy and saying, "Did you hear about Jennie?" This was my story, and I wanted it told in my voice. I wanted to be able to shape the way the story was presented, and shift it, slightly, with each telling, the way you do when you tell something over and over again, until you own each stop and start. I wanted to hear all the sharp intakes of breath and the words that made people gasp. In those responses, I would hear the fact that I was important, that this was big, and that I was alive.

I had often talked with Lisa about the power of telling your own story. Her doctoral thesis was about how autistic people speak about themselves and, through their limited speech, form an identity. She had spent hours in research labs charting conversations and listening for the rhythms and patterns in the way her patients spoke. She listened for the way people protected, defined, and healed themselves as they spoke—whether they were autistic people struggling to communicate, Vietnam vets struggling for a national identity, or even mothers struggling to maintain their own voice amid the clamor of their kids. Whenever I felt that my work as a writer was futile or impossible to combine with motherhood, Lisa would always encourage me without hesitation because she felt mothers' stories were so important to tell.

I kept my mouth shut when Rob was on the phone because of his mother. It was the one thing I felt frantic about—how vulnerable and horrified Rob must feel, how unfair this all was to him. It was the one thing that seemed as big as the fact that I had cancer—the one reality I could see outside myself: the fact that Rob's mother had died of breast cancer and now his wife had it, too. Rob himself didn't seem fazed by this parallel; he seemed the way he always seemed—steady and ready to face whatever had to be faced. I'd already waited six years for him to fall apart over his parents' deaths and it hadn't happened yet. He wasn't the fall-apart kind of guy. Letting him tell my story was my way of apologizing for his having to rise to the occasion of breast cancer yet again, and my way of thanking him.

The only time I hesitated talking about my cancer was with my kids. I knew that the "bad news from the doctor" story would only buy me a little time. My kids—like all kids—are insightful, intuitive, and curious. They would quickly figure out that something was wrong and they would demand to know what it was. I didn't want to lie. Part of my job is to teach them the importance of honesty, but it's also my job to protect them, and by telling them that I had cancer, I would be admitting that the world is a scary and dangerous place that's largely out of our control. Was that something they needed to hear at ages three and a half and seven? In a perfect world, no. But our world was no longer perfect. The challenge was to tell them that I had cancer in a way that would make them feel that they were still safe, and I knew it wasn't going to be easy.

Carlyn, who was just about to turn seven, knew enough about breast cancer to know it can kill you. Rob's mother, Jean, died when Carlyn was only a year old. We traveled to Houston for her last days and stayed in a hotel room near her hospice. We took Carlyn to Jean's room each day to sit and to watch and to wait. Jean looked like she was sleeping, drawing slower and slower breaths as each day wore on, growing colder and colder in her limbs. Carlyn usually just wandered around the room and looked out the window and sat in our laps and drank juice. The day Jean's last breath came, however, she stepped through the doorway into the room, stopped, and said, "Bye-bye." No one had told her that Jean had died or even what, exactly, death was; Carlyn had simply understood.

We'd often shared with Carlyn and Emily the story of Carlyn's instinctive understanding of death. It was an inspiring and spiritual story of intuition. Now, however, it was a story that haunted us. What if Carlyn asked if I was going to die? What would Rob and I say? As far as we knew, the answer was no. I had an early cancer that the doctors believed was confined to the breast. My odds of surviving were very good. But when it comes to cancer, no one really knows anything. One tiny cell could be loose in your body, searching for a favorable place to rest, ready to replicate into infinity. Technically, the correct answer is yes—I'm going to die, but maybe not now, maybe not of this cancer. Rob and I decided to say no.

Two days after I had heard the news, we sat the girls down on the green couch by the fireplace. It's a spot we usually reserve for important family events, such as discussions about dinnertime manners or a change in the chore chart. That's about as serious as things had ever been with us.

"The bad news I got from the doctor the other day," I began, "is that I have cancer in my breast."

Before I could take a breath and go on, Carlyn jumped in. "Are you going to die like Daddy's mom?"

I smiled wryly. What a clever girl she was to make that connection and what clever parents we were to have known she would.

"No," Rob said. "Grandma Jean had a bad kind of cancer. Mom has a good kind." These were the words we'd decided to use to reduce the reality of early detection to the lowest common denominator.

"Phew." Carlyn sighed, swiping her hand across her forehead. That was all she wanted or needed to know—if I was going to die. Having been reassured that I wasn't, she turned her attention to the piping on the pillows, to the zipper of the slipcover, and finally to the padded back of the couch, where she climbed, perched, and lolled.

Emily, who was only three and a half but has a more naturally sympathetic nature, was more inquisitive. What was cancer? How were they going to get it out of me? Was it going to hurt?

We ended up drawing her a picture of dots the size of a pencil point, and then erasing them to show her what the doctors would do. We assured her that even if it hurt, I would be okay. She carefully drew her own dots and practiced erasing them from the page.

"I'm sorry you have cancer, Mama," she said, her little forehead creased.

"Me, too," I said.

⁂

In the days when it was typical for cancer to be kept secret, and in cultures and families where it is still considered taboo, women probably thought they were the only people on the face of the planet with the disease. The loneliness must have been chilling. My telling everyone my story, on the other hand, resulted in all of them telling me theirs. Everyone had a sister or an aunt or a mother, an in-law, a colleague or a neighbor, a roommate or a friend or a daughter who had been diagnosed. I heard story after story of lumps and tests, surgeries and treatments. Sometimes people's stories got out in front of them and before they could stop themselves and remember that they were talking to someone newly diagnosed, they blurted out tales of recurrences and death. There were days when I heard so many stories that I wondered if my ears had previously been plugged. I'd seen the headlines and the magazine articles about breast cancer ("Is it an epidemic?" "Can it be cured?"), but I hadn't heard the stories.

Some cancer patients hate it when they're told stories of other people's sickness and death. One woman I know began to reply to these tragedies with the blunt comment "You're going to die, too." She found that that was an effective way to shut people up. I found, however, that I didn't want to turn off the stories, even the ones that ended badly. It was as if by telling me the stories they knew about breast cancer, people were saying, "This isn't so foreign," "This isn't so bad," "You're not alone."

Sometimes the things people say turn out to be unspeakable. I know a breast cancer patient whose sister said to her in a burst of anger, "Your having breast cancer raises the odds of my getting it by a *third*." Another woman's father never spoke to her again after the conversation in which she told him she was ill. You don't always get the reaction you want when you tell everyone you know, but at least you can decide whom to ignore. At least you have the chance of hearing stories, getting advice, and gaining support. What we know now that we didn't know in the days when cancer was whispered about is that it's a chronic disease. You don't necessarily have it, get rid of it, and move on. You live with the idea of it, the reality of it, and the possibility of it for the rest of your life, even if it's not technically present. Having the support of your friends and family can be a critical component to your health—like elderly people who have a dog to keep them company, to sit by their side, to let them know each day that they're not in this world without a friend.

⁓

The last person I told my news to was Lisa. I wrote her a short card telling her what had occurred, and how. "You saved my life," I said, "and I wanted to thank you."

She wrote back immediately:

I'm praying that you caught it early enough to make a difference. I'm praying that you won't have to have chemo. I love you dearly. Be strong.

Lesson #3

It's Important to Eat Cake

There's nothing like a life-threatening illness to make you think about what's important. Even if you're not going to die anytime soon, the thought of the possibility of death is enough to get your mind to focus. You grab on to the things in your life that are a blessing and a privilege to be a part of, and you tend to let go of the things that aren't. Treatment sometimes makes it impossible to enjoy these things—but the hope is that treatment is only temporary.

My doctors—the oncologist and surgeon I'd chosen—recommended that I go to the second-opinion clinic at UCLA's Revlon Breast Center because the pathology on my cancer wasn't entirely clear. The cells themselves looked as though they were confined to the milk ducts, but because of their aggressive nuclei, there was some question as to whether or not there had been microinvasions outside of the ducts. They wanted to make sure they were treating the right cancer. The clinic is a one-day marathon in which patients sit in an examining room and over the course of six hours see a surgeon, a radiologist, an oncologist, a pathologist, a psychologist, and a nurse—and all their student attendants. At the end of the day, the specialists meet and send you home with a recommended course of action for treating your cancer. The day I was able to reserve an appointment at the clinic happened to be Carlyn's seventh birthday.

Although I had been in denial about the biopsy, I was not in denial about my disease. I knew I had been lucky to find it early, but I also knew that the clock was ticking and that no one knows cancer's timetable. The odds weren't particularly likely that I was going to die from this cancer anytime soon or perhaps anytime at all, but the fact remained that I could die. This was a new and novel idea for me and I'm still amazed that we don't all wake up every day and believe in our own deaths. We can go days, weeks, months, and years feeling immortal. Our flesh is so fragile—heir to a thousand natural shocks—yet our spirits are so strong. We get up every day and believe in our own life, until we're hit over the head with a test result or almost hit by a semi truck on a freeway overpass. There was no way I was going to stay home from UCLA to eat birthday cake and play balloon volleyball—but that didn't make the decision any easier. Carlyn's birthday matters so much to me, not only because I get to celebrate the many ways in which she has grown and changed, but also because I get to celebrate the fact that her birth no longer haunts me.

∽

Everyone always says that having a healthy baby is the most important outcome of birth and I believe that to be true. I've known people who did not get that result, and their sadness and pain is deep and never-ending. I got a healthy baby, for whom I give thanks every day, but I had a traumatic experience doing so. I had a long labor followed by a C-section, and the epidural never worked correctly. I felt the sharp edge of the surgeon's knife as it sliced into my belly. I screamed for her to stop and retched from the pain. When, minutes later, she handed me my healthy little girl, I shook my head no. I was too traumatized to hold her. Over the next three days, Carlyn was nurtured and named by my husband, and held to my breast to nurse, but all I remember are the waves of nausea from the narcotics, the waves of pain from the incision, and the waves of resentment that people were fussing so much over my baby and not enough over me.

Guilt, resentment, and confusion plagued me for more than a year. They call it the baby blues, but postpartum depression is not nearly so coy as that term implies. I wondered if I had made a mistake by having a baby and at the same time I worried that I had caused irreparable damage by my inability to hold her or name her or care about her in the first three days of her life. I was reluctant to leave the house because it panicked me to be out for a walk or over at a friend's house when Carlyn fell asleep; I lived for the respite from resentment and responsibility that her sleep gave me and when I didn't get it, I felt exhausted and overwhelmed. Just the sight of Rob leaving for work in the morning—a seemingly carefree day ahead of him—would bring me to tears.

I cared for Carlyn during the first year of her life—and I cared for her well—but it took me that long to learn to love her. I've never fought so hard to build a relationship and I felt as if Carlyn fought right along with me. We wanted to love each other and, over time, we figured out how. We built a secure, strong, joyous relationship, and she is now a constant and daily delight to me. My love for my second daughter, Emily, was, in contrast, instant. It was easy. It was vastly different, and I treasure it for different reasons. On Carlyn's birthday each year, my mother asks me if I still remember the events of the day. She believes that birthdays are, in many ways, more of a celebration for the mother who labored than for the child who simply arrived. I always nod; I remember. And I like to celebrate how far we've come.

⚬⚬

The minute I decided to go to UCLA and not be with Carlyn on her birthday, I leaped into action to compensate for my absence. I baked cupcakes for her soccer

practice that day, tied ribbons onto the laminated book-
marks we'd made for her to hand out to her classmates,
and asked who, of all the people in the world besides me
and Dad, she most wanted to be with and what, out of all
the things to do, she most wanted to do. Her answers
were simple and easy to arrange: she wanted to be with
Emily and our neighbors, the Honakers, and she wanted
to go to Burger King.

"You understand why Daddy and I can't be with you,
don't you?" I asked.

"You have to see the doctors about getting your cancer out," she said, slightly annoyed. She'd heard me the
first time, and she was unfazed.

"And you know I'll be here to do your party on Friday. Nothing will keep me from doing that."

"You said that, Mom," she said.

"And you know I wish I had another choice, right?"

"Mom!" she cried, exasperated. She was excited
about cupcakes at soccer and hamburgers for dinner and
a long day playing with the neighbors. She wanted me to
leave and get on with it.

I actually wanted the exact same thing—to stop
obsessing about my kids, to be free to focus on myself—
but it was too hard to make that kind of paradigm shift.
I was wired to be their primary caretaker—to beat the
cupcake batter, peel the apple, referee the fights, ice the
bruises, find the favorite pair of pants that never came
out of the laundry, listen to the complaint that someone
at school had said something mean, answer the question

about time or heaven or the meaning of "colossal," and explain why we often have to do things we'd really rather not do—and I went right on doing it all. Sometimes I prayed for nothing as hard as my kids' bedtime.

On Wednesday morning, Rob and I dropped off the kids with the Honakers and drove an hour up the 405 to UCLA. The whole time on the freeway, I kept saying to Rob, "Do you think she'll be okay?" "Do you think she was sad?"

"Yes," he answered. "No," he answered. "She'll be fine," he said.

At the Revlon Center, we were led, along with twelve other groups of patients and their partners, into a conference room, where we were given the guidelines for the day. It was hard not to look at the other groups of nervous people sitting around the big wooden table and on cushioned benches along the walls. Was that attractive older woman the patient or was it the younger woman who looked just like her? Did that husband merely agree to drive his wife here today or was he an involved and loving partner? Was the woman in the purple dress going to be here to celebrate Christmas? I wondered if Rob saw his mother in any of the older women sitting around us.

Rob held my hand until my name was called and we were led to an examining room, where the specialists would come in rotation to see us. We sat there reading our breast books and the stacks of pages we'd printed off the Internet, and then the head nurse came in.

"If you're going to have breast cancer," she said, "this

is the kind of cancer you want to have. You know that, right? You know how lucky you are to have caught it early?"

We nodded.

"Let me see," she said, looking at my chart. "You're thirty-five. Do you have any family history of the disease?"

"No," I said.

She looked up. "How did you happen to go for a mammogram?" she asked.

I told my story about Lisa's illness and my fearful imagination, the trip to the family practitioner, and the fortuitous mammogram. I stopped short of telling the nurse how Lisa had just celebrated her thirty-fifth birthday and how I had sent her a copy of *Pilgrim at Tinker Creek* with a bookmark on the page with the quote she liked that begins "I am a frayed and nibbled survivor in a fallen world and I am getting along." I said nothing about how, at her party, Lisa's guests had helped her work on the mosaic tile wall she was building in her garden, and how, after they left, Lisa sat in the sun and moved around the tiles whose placement she didn't like, and how I hadn't been able to go to the party. The nurse wrote a few notes on the chart, asked dozens of other questions about my medical history, and said the radiologist would be in next.

Minutes later a young man in a white lab coat, brown loafers, and glasses came in. The way he held his clipboard so determinedly, his shoulders so unnaturally erect, told us that he was still a student. He said that he was a radiology intern and that he'd do the patient interview for the radiologist, who would be in shortly.

We nodded.

"No family history, no tumor," he said. "What made you go in for a mammogram?"

I smiled and told him the story about Lisa's illness and my fearful imagination, the trip to the family practitioner, and the fortuitous mammogram. He wrote something on my chart and proceeded to ask me many of the same questions the nurse had asked. When he was done with the interview, he explained to us the way radiation worked to stop cancer in the breast, and how the skin would burn, and how a portion of the lung would be nuked. I got the feeling he had recently mastered this material, but he had it down pat. While we waited for the doctor, we asked the intern as many questions as we could think of about how radiation reduces the risk of the cancer recurring and what side effects I could expect.

The radiologist soon came in. He was a large man with gray hair and he settled himself ponderously on the swivel stool at the side of the examining table, halfway across the room from where Rob and I sat. He barked at the young intern to see if the student had done his job, and when he was satisfied that his protégé had asked all the right questions in the right way, he turned to me.

"What's a thirty-five-year-old woman with no family history and no tumor doing getting a mammogram?"

I wanted to say "Because I *felt* like it," but I reminded

myself that these people were here to help me, so I told my story about Lisa's illness and my fearful imagination, the trip to the family practitioner, and the fortuitous mammogram. When I was done, the radiologist let out a kind of guffaw. "I just made a recommendation to a rather large HMO that women without a history don't need mammograms before they're forty."

It was unclear whether this was a confession or a comment of irony. None of the other four people in the small room said anything in reply. The radiologist asked me some additional questions about my history, explained that the type of cancer I had tended to recur more than most, said "That's why we like to swat it hard," and then walked out.

Every single person who came in to see me that day in that room asked me why I'd gotten a mammogram. Every intern, every resident, every doctor, every nurse. By the time the day was over, and I had my second opinion in hand—which confirmed my doctor's opinion to do a lumpectomy, hope for a clean margin of healthy tissue around the cancerous tissue, and do six weeks of radiation to kill any cells that were left behind—I'd told my story more than a dozen times.

∽

There was bumper-to-bumper traffic on the way home. Rob and I sat silently in the car, listening to golden oldies, inching our way home, totally spent. When we finally knocked on the Honakers' door at 8:00, Carlyn and Emily were snuggled up on the couch with Sarah and Kyle, watching *101 Dalmatians*. They barely even looked up when we walked in and called out for the birthday girl.

"They're pretty tired," Denise explained. "We had a treasure hunt after school and then the soccer thing, and Burger King—well, you can see what Burger King was like." I looked to where she was pointing. There were three huge shopping bags piled with presents.

"What's all this?" Rob asked.

"A few friends met us for dinner to surprise Carlyn."

Carlyn piped up from the couch. "Cody was there and Geoffrey and Allison and Alexandra. The girls chased the boys."

I felt so grateful to Denise for making Carlyn's day special. I was overwhelmed with gratitude—and I was jealous. It wasn't so much that Carlyn could so easily be made happy by someone else's love and effort. It was that I had missed the look on her face, the thrill in her voice, the sticky fingers, the torn wrapping paper, and the happy taunting the girls made to the boys to get them to play chase. I had missed the chance to share my child's birthday cake.

"How were the cupcakes?" I asked.

"Smushed," Carlyn said. "Can I have another one?"

"She already had two or three," Denise explained.

"Four," Carlyn corrected.

"Sure," I said, "let's have a cupcake." We lifted the tinfoil off the shoebox and lifted out the leftover cupcakes. They were indeed smashed and sticky and cloying.

Eating one, I convinced myself that if I died—from cancer or from a flowerpot falling on my head—my children would be okay. I believed that they would find love in the world, and strength and solace and guidance and someone to share birthday cake with—because what else could I possibly believe?

Courage Doesn't Always Dress in Camouflage

Breast cancer survivors have, by definition, over-come an insidious, life-threatening disease, and in a huge number of cases, they've done so with strength, grace, and courage. You may not think you've been courageous, but remember that courage doesn't always look the way you think it does. Courage can be getting out of bed every morning or remembering to say thank you to everyone who knocks on your door with food or flowers. In some cases, courage can even be wearing a beautiful dress.

The Saturday after Carlyn's birthday there was a silent auction at our church. I'd been on the committee that was putting the fund-raising party together and I knew what a great event it was going to be—great music, great food, a roomful of people feeling festive and spending money for a good cause. Our theme was "Black and White, Starry Night"—which was meant to be somewhat heavenly, somewhat elegant, and a clue that the dress code was anything black and white. For months, while working on the invitations and soliciting donations, I had envisioned myself wearing my favorite black-tie outfit— a long black velvet skirt with a cut-velvet bodysuit top. The top was mesh with a pattern of velvet roses scattered across it, and I wore it with a black bustier. The bustier, though technically as solid as a piece of armor, had the effect of making the outfit look like an elegant, formfitting, strapless gown. My husband loved it, I always felt grown-up when I wore it—wise and worldly and sexy— and it was black as night. But I was scheduled to have a lumpectomy five days after the event—a procedure where a breast surgeon takes a wedge of tissue from your breast, as if from an orange—and somehow a black dress didn't feel right. I realized that this would be the last public and formal event I'd ever attend with both my breasts still intact.

I have, over the years, grown rather attached to my breasts. When I was in high school and college, I didn't think much about them—they were average B-cup breasts, so what was there to think? They didn't bounce too much when I played tennis, they filled out any dress or shirt I chose to wear, they became marginally tender once a month, and they were one of the primary reasons my boyfriend was able to say he liked my curves. The process of pregnancy, breast-feeding, and motherhood, however, gave my breasts a whole new level of value. It made them, for one thing, a cup size bigger. They were plump and full, which made that same boyfriend—now my husband—pay even more attention, which was flattering and fun. Making babies also made my breasts functional. I breast-fed both my children, for nine months each, and was proud that I could produce all those antibodies, all that concentrated protein.

I was three years past breast-feeding when I learned I had cancer, and down a breast size from finally losing the weight of childbearing, so my breasts were, in some ways, past their prime. I didn't need them to please a man because Rob now knew that there was far more to me than just my curves. For all practical intents and purposes, I didn't need my breasts to go on living a happy and healthy life, but the lumpectomy was still going to do them damage—and damage to your own flesh isn't something you can just offhandedly accept. My breast would have a dent. The nipple might be distorted. The whole thing might cave in like a rotten cantaloupe.

"At least it's only a lumpectomy," Rob said one night, while we were sitting in the hot tub in our backyard.

"What do you mean 'only'?" I demanded.

"I looked at those pictures in the book," he confessed, referring to the pages in the breast book that were outside of the sections dedicated to lumpectomy, "and those mastectomy scars are nasty. The ones that aren't rebuilt?"

"Are you saying you're only interested in a perfect

breast?" I pushed. "Because I'm not going to have a perfect breast."

"No—I'm just saying that it'd be hard to look at a
mastectomy scar for the rest of my life."

I wanted to tell Rob that I hated him for what he'd
just said—that I thought it was egotistical and insensitive
and male—but the thing was that I agreed, so much so
that I feared it might be hard to look at a *lumpectomy* scar
for the rest of my life. "Well, if it were me getting a mastectomy, I might not reconstruct, either," I argued. "I
mean, it is what it is, so why bother to pretend otherwise?"

I stood up and reached for my towel. "I don't know
what your problem is with scars," I spat, as I climbed out
of the tub, "but you better get over it—fast."

∽

The night of the party started out at a frantic pace. Rob
had to be at the church early to help with the valet parking, the Honakers were going to follow me in their car,
and I first had to run the kids across town to the baby-
sitter. I was left with just ten minutes to get dressed. I ran
into the house, went to pull out the black skirt, the
mesh bodysuit, and the industrial-strength bustier—and
stopped. Hanging next to the black velvet, encased in
cool dry-cleaner plastic, was a long, luxurious raspberry-
red Nicole Miller gown with a deep V neck in front and
a deeper V in back. I'd never worn it.

I bought the dress with my sister, Laura, for no good reason, on sale at a little boutique in Yarmouth, Maine. We were there at the end of a vacation. It was getting late and the kids were getting hungry, but Laura insisted that we take forty-five minutes to shop the big sale at a boutique she had discovered on her visit the summer before. We left the kids with their dads and skidded into the store right before closing, determined to find some deals.

We scoured the sale racks and crammed into the dressing room, trading outfits to see which clothes looked better on which person, bickering over who would get the half-price Tencel shorts and who would get the perfect straw hat. I put on the Nicole Miller gown just for fun, stepped out of the dressing room to preen in front of the mirror, and was met with the stares of every woman in the shop.

"That dress was made for you," one woman said.

"Do they have a size eight?" another woman asked.

"You're buying it," my sister declared.

The dress was perfect—a simple '40s movie star dress that was curvy in exactly the same places that I was. I had absolutely nowhere to wear such a dress, but I bought it, carted it back to California, sent it to the dry cleaner's, and stuck it in the back of my closet. It'd been there for two years.

Reaching into my closet on the night of the church party, the week after my cancer diagnosis, I made a split-second decision: I was going to wear the red dress.

Because of its deep V's, I couldn't wear a regular bra. I supposed I could wear the bustier, but standing there alone in my bedroom, I thought, What's the point?

I slipped the dress over my bare body and felt the cool glide of the satin lining fall from my shoulders to my ankles. I felt the fabric brush against my breasts. I pinned up my hair, put on some bright red lipstick, and took off—to be the only woman wearing a red dress in a roomful of black and white.

I have never in my life been a woman who turned heads. I have never felt confident enough in my looks to carry myself in such a way that I would. That night, however, I felt like the most beautiful woman in the world. I felt wholly alive in that red dress, and people must have picked up on that electricity, as if it were a series of signals or a fragrance. Men and women alike, people I knew and people I didn't know, came up to me to tell me how spectacular I looked, what a gorgeous dress I had on, and how I seemed to glow. I loved the feeling of swishing around the room, feeling the weight of that dress as it draped to the floor, feeling it cool and clean on my bare breasts, which for that one night, anyway, were still mine.

Everyone in that room who knew me knew that I had just been diagnosed with cancer. The Sunday before, every hymn we sang in church made me cry, convulsively, so that I'd had to walk out of the service every ten minutes. But not one of my fellow parishioners mentioned my diagnosis the night of the party. It wasn't as if they were afraid or being sensitive or polite. It was as if my wearing the red dress prohibited the very idea of breast cancer, like a shield of armor or a vest of Mylar.

A few days later, however, I got a call from the head of the party committee, thanking me for my help—which I'd abruptly stopped giving two weeks earlier. "We finally got everything cleaned up," she said, "and you were the hottest topic of discussion around the dish-drying rack."

"Me?" I said, thinking of the way church ladies chatter and gossip, and wondering what I could possibly have done.

"You were the most beautiful woman in the room that night, Jennie, and the most courageous. A lot of women in your shoes wouldn't have even shown up, let alone worn that dress."

Courageous? I thought. Courageous? So *that* was what courage felt like—that rush of judgment to know just what to do—or wear—that sense of satisfaction that nothing—not even cancer—was going to stand in my way of feeling utterly confident, that sweet perfume of feeling completely and totally alive. If that was courage, it suited me as well as the red dress.

Lesson #5

Daddy Can't Always Keep
the Monsters Away,
but He Can Fold the Laundry

Cancer gives people a great opportunity to rise to the occasion—to be present, to be understanding, to tell you all the things they never said before. The lesson is to let them.

My dad has never been a very hands-on kind of parent. He was always more likely to be off running a river or climbing a mountain than he was to see me play in the tennis final or head off to the prom. He was, true to form, on his tugboat, *Forevergreen*, in the San Francisco Bay when my lumpectomy was scheduled for a Wednesday in the middle of November.

"Should I come home?" he kept asking from his crackling cell phone. "Do you need my help?" I pictured him pacing my suburban home, yearning for wide-open spaces, dreaming of the Golden Gate Bridge. "If you want to be here, I'd like you to come," I said, "but I'll be okay without you."

"Mom's not coming?" he asked—for the third, fourth, and fifth time. My mother was taking my niece Caroline on a long-planned trip to England for her tenth birthday. My lumpectomy had been scheduled for the earliest possible time Dr. Peter could do it, and this time happened to coincide with the trip.

"She's not coming," I said to my dad. "She'll be here Monday."

"But Rob will be there?" he asked.

"He'll be here," I answered. "He's taking the day off from work and a friend from church is going to stay with him at the hospital all day. The kids will spend the night with Lori."

"And you don't want me to come? I could dock the boat in Tiburon and fly down," he mused, "or we could trailer the boat down and be there—let's see—on Friday. That wouldn't put us in L.A. for the surgery, but we could be there the day after. We could be there until your mother comes back on Monday." The "we" referred to his wife and my friend, Honeydew. Honeydew had been an important support during the births of my two daughters. She had also survived ovarian cancer at the age of twenty, at a time when they didn't even have chemo to increase the chances of survival, and I felt certain she would go anywhere on earth I needed her to be, but I got the impression the decision-making on this visit was my dad's. He was the one who needed to be here.

"Look, Dad," I said finally, just to stop him from fretting, "why don't you just come."

∽

My surgery was on a Wednesday afternoon. On Wednesday morning, I took the kids to school, called Lori to make sure she knew exactly when and where to pick them up, then went out into the garden and clipped away everything that was dead or dying or out of control. I clipped away my garden's cancer, and went for my lumpectomy smelling of rosemary.

Rob drove me to the office of the radiologist, who performed a procedure called a needle localization. This is a low-tech trick that frames the cancerous tissue so the surgeon knows what to cut out. The radiologist localizes the cancer because she's the one who knows where it is. What she did was this: peered at my mammogram films, kneeled on the ground in front of me, took three very long needles and stuck them in my breast, then squeezed my breast in a mammogram machine to make sure she got it right. There was no anesthesia because anesthesia can blur what the surgeon sees. The needles were just stuck in, unceremoniously, as if what we were doing was some kind of black magic. I gasped—but was amazed that what seemed like a bar-

baric procedure wasn't anywhere near as painful as it had a right to be.

"Are you okay?" the radiologist asked, after each needle.

I nodded for one and two. After the third, I told the doctor I'd had a facial at a fancy spa the day before because I thought it would be relaxing. I didn't know they would dig at my pores as if drilling for oil. "The facial hurt more than this did," I said.

She laughed.

In the lull that followed, I asked, "Did you get it right? The needles, I mean. Are they in the right spot?"

"I got it right," she said, with such confidence and assurance that I sailed out of the room, despite the needles protruding from my breast.

Rob drove me to the hospital, but we were afraid to touch—to hold hands, let alone to hug. We were afraid the needles would shift out of place—which would not only hurt, but could also ruin my chances for getting every last bit of cancer out. Rob sat next to me in the waiting room, stood next to me when I was given a bed, and listened intently while the anesthesiologist and I discussed my body's peculiar reaction to anesthesia during my children's births and the options for which drugs to give me now.

Our minister, Ginna, arrived a few minutes before I was to be wheeled into the OR and asked the nurses if they wanted to pray. I was embarrassed at the audacity of the request—thinking *they* would be embarrassed, thinking prayer should be private, or if public, that it should be in a place designated for prayer—but the nurses nodded, formed a circle around me, and prayed. We prayed that the doctors and nurses would do the jobs for which they had been trained, for the miracle of medicine, and for my body's healthy response. Tears were streaming down my face when they wheeled me away because it seemed like so much to ask.

∽

Rob was holding my hand when I woke up, and as far as I remember, he held it for the next five hours. That's how long it took me to come out of the anesthesia. Other people came and went from the recovery room like characters in a fast-forwarded movie, but I just stayed, fixed to my bed, woozy and nauseous and half-alert. A Lakers game was on the television, which I watched with a dazed, partial understanding. At one point I insisted on getting up to go to the bathroom because I thought if I could make it to the bathroom, I could make it home. I sat up and threw up instead. It was a long day.

I slept that night in my own bed, immensely grateful that the girls weren't asleep at the other end of the hall—poised to have to pee in the middle of the night and programmed to leap out of bed and jump in next to me somewhere close to sunrise. The next morning, Rob got up and went back to work and my friend Jo came to care for me. I was too tired to sleep, so I sat on the couch and thumbed through old copies of her *Martha Stewart* magazines. Jo cooked—both lunch and dinner—while I read, and before she left, she set the table with flowers and stemware.

My breast was wrapped in a thick waterproof bandage so it was impossible to see what it looked like. I stared at it in the shower that first night, wondering what it would look like underneath. I wondered especially where the nipple was, since I couldn't quite tell. I worried that it had disappeared, but I laughed the worry off, knowing they'd just taken a small slice of breast, a cross-section, a little piece of tissue, the few cells of cancer they'd found on the mammogram.

My dad and Honeydew arrived the following morning with a cooler full of picnic food—salmon and soybeans, bean dip and turkey roll-ups.

As I lay on my bed with a bandage on my breast and painkillers in my veins, my dad sat on the floor and folded laundry, making neat piles of my little girls' clothes. I was in the bed, there was laundry in the basket, and there was nowhere my dad could go to bike or ski or run. We talked about driving across deserts, which we'd often done when I was a child, and leading people into the wilderness, which my dad has done all his life, both for his job as a professor of environmental studies and because he loves to show people the country he loves. I told my dad something I'd never told him before, which was that his leadership had made it hard for me to feel any sense of responsibility on all those wilderness trips.

He led the way a conductor leads an orchestra. My role was to follow and be wowed by his performance. I wished sometimes that he had let me discover the wonders and make the mistakes myself.

In reply, he told me a story, which is his style. He told me that the day before, he had cried at a TV commercial for an insurance company. My dad is a man who does not show a lot of emotion, and he told me that he'd broken down over a television ad. The commercial showed a little girl who was afraid of the dark because of the monsters under the bed and a dad who comes on and says, "I'll always protect you." My dad wished he could do this for me, and he cried because he couldn't.

I looked up at the end of the story and noticed that he was making a neat little pile of my underwear, which I usually just cram into a drawer. "You're folding my underwear," I blurted, stunned to see his strong, thick, sunburned hands working with the clean white cotton.

He looked down at his hands and shrugged. "I'm just glad to be here," he said.

⁓

I was sure that the monsters were gone from my body. When I was first pregnant with Carlyn—so early that it was too early to do even a home test—I remember going to a yoga class that met in a building something like a tree house, cantilevered out among the pine trees on the side of a hill. Sunlight streamed in the windows, and we all stretched on the ground on fraying red mats. I lay flat on my mat, directing each part of my body to relax as the instructor called out its name. When she called out "belly and reproductive organs," I focused on my lower abdomen, directed all my powers of observation there, and knew without a doubt that I had conceived a child.

I had that same unshakable faith that there was no cancer in my breast. I had focused on it, prayed about it, searched the depths of my cells and my soul, and I knew that there was no cancer left in my breast. When people asked how I was, I'd answer, "Cancer free." When people asked what was going to happen next, I'd say, "Radiation, starting January third, just to be on the safe side." When my dad asked whether he should stay through Monday, when my mom was due in from England and when we were scheduled to hear the news from the pathologist, I thought about the way my mom and dad would be so attentive to each other's words and actions, and the way they would be wound just a little more tightly in each others' presence and the way they would quietly vie to show that they were the parent who was most relieved at the good news. "I don't think so," I said. "Why don't I just call when we hear."

He put a bottle of champagne in the refrigerator and headed back to his boat in the bay, as planned. I was sorry to see him go.

∽

My mom called early in the morning from Kennedy Airport saying she was on her way to L.A. I called the doctor at eleven o'clock and was told that the pathology reports weren't in. I called again around 2:00 and was told that the reports still weren't in. The girls came home from school and I asked their friend Sarah, from next door, to come over to keep them occupied. I didn't have the nerves or the will to work a *Little Mermaid* puzzle or play the mean headmaster in an elaborate game of orphans. My mom arrived at my house at 4:00, bustling and nervous. "Still haven't heard," I said cheerfully, as if there'd been some perfectly understandable delay—a Monday morning glitch akin to the coffee machine breaking down. But when your emotions are in a heightened state, you learn to read minuscule signs, and as sure as I was that they'd gotten all the cancer out, I was sure that if the news was good, I would have already been told. Someone somewhere in Dr. Peter's office was holding back information, which could only mean that the news wasn't good. When Dr. Peter called around 4:30, the kids were playing dress-up in the living room and my mother was unpacking fruit tea from Fortnum and Mason in the kitchen. I took the phone into my office at the back of the house, where I could be sure to hear every word.

"I hate to tell you over the phone," Dr. Peter said, "but they've only done thirteen of the thirty-one slides and twelve of the thirteen are positive. We took a large piece of tissue and it's full of cancer. I'd like you to call my office tomorrow and make an appointment for you and Rob to come in and talk to me about a mastectomy."

I must have said something—made some sort of guttural noise. "You can swear if you want to," Dr. Peter said. "It's an appropriate time to swear. It's really shitty news."

I smiled, grateful for his words even as the terror of what they conveyed hit me. I started to cry, and repeated, "It's really shitty news."

He went on to explain how they were very surprised to see so much cancer around the margins of the affected tissue—how the mammogram hadn't showed any signs of that. He explained that if there are only one or two dirty points on the margin, they may be able to go back in and scrape out a few extra millimeters of tissue, but that with decidedly dirty margins like mine, there was little choice but to take the whole breast.

As soon as I hung up the phone, I dropped my head in my hands and howled. The monsters were still under the bed.

The kids came running, again, when they heard my sobs—Carlyn, Emily, and Sarah. They made a big game out of bringing me Kleenex and asking if I was okay. I kept shaking my head, so they kept bringing me more Kleenex and then they started bringing me stuffed bears and fleece blankets. My mom tried to contain them in another room, but they would not be held back. When Denise came to the door to take Sarah home a half hour later, I said, "The news was bad." She hugged me and we cried. "I'm so sorry Sarah was here," I blurted. "When you get home, tell her I'm sorry."

⁓

I immediately did the same thing I did the first time I got bad news: I called everyone I knew. This time, however, it didn't buoy me up. All it did was make me cry each time I had to admit that my body had betrayed my mind. I'd been wrong—they didn't get the cancer out.

I knew immediately that I needed more help than my friends and family could provide—more specific understanding of what a mastectomy was all about, more professional counseling as to the decisions that had to be made, more detailed stories of women who were going through the same thing at the same time. As my mom cleaned up the breakfast dishes, I picked up the phone and called the local branch of The Wellness Community, the nonprofit support center made famous by Gilda Radner. The mother of a woman I sometimes wrote for had given me the number weeks ago, but I hadn't called because I didn't think I needed the support of a group of strangers—strangers who were probably angry, bitter, and scared.

Lisa and I had laughed, in fact, about the whole support group impetus, and how well-wishers always get around to suggesting it. "My social worker keeps trying to get me to go to a lung cancer group," she told me one day, "so I can face my mortality. But everyone in those groups is old and sick and dying. That's not exactly how I want to face my mortality."

I laughed. I doubt if I knew anyone as conscious of her mortality and how to face it as Lisa. At her father's funeral two years before, I sat in the Santa Barbara Mission—the same chapel where Lisa had been married—and listened to various luminaries eulogize this gentle, insightful, and learned man. After them, Lisa spoke about how her dad used to e-mail her every day to tell her a joke, give her advice, or rave about the Swedish meatballs he'd had for lunch. "We'll have to find a new way of having a relationship now," she said in a voice that did not waver, "one that doesn't have to do with phone calls, e-mails, and visits home but with faith and prayer. I'll have to find a new way of listening."

I wasn't facing my mortality just yet. I was facing a mastectomy. But being part of a support group was, suddenly, how I needed to face it.

"I'm calling to find out about breast cancer support groups," I said to the woman who answered the phone at The Wellness Community.

"Have you had an interview?" she asked.

"An interview?" I repeated. "No."

"Have you been to a newcomers meeting?"

"No," I said.

"Are you under forty?"

"Yes," I said, feeling pleased to have qualified for something. "I am."

"We have a young couples group tomorrow night,

which would qualify as a newcomers meeting. There's a newly diagnosed breast cancer group starting next Tuesday. A caregiver group meets at the same time."

"Oh," I said, feeling immensely relieved. "That's good."

⁂

There was a woman at the young couples meeting—a loud, lusty, bald woman in a pristine white turban and comfortable shoes sitting next to a curly-haired, handsome man in a red polo shirt—who announced to the group that she had just found out her breast cancer had metastasized to her brain. She'd already had a double mastectomy, bone marrow and stem cell transplants, and something like eight different courses of chemo. She was having seizures, so the doctors had just taken away her driver's license. She'd been crying for two days straight. She was twenty-eight years old. Her husband spoke after she did, and explained how there had been a time when he thought his life would include a picket fence, children, and good times with the woman he'd married. He now understood that his life was about his wife's cancer.

I couldn't take my eyes off this woman. I can't even remember her name now, but she sat on the couch across from me, cracking jokes about chemo brain and offering advice to other people in the room on how to handle their pain. She was beautiful. She was soulful. She was more alive than anyone I'd ever seen, and she filled me with thoughts of Lisa.

I was sure that Lisa was like the woman in the white turban, in public anyway. Lisa told me that women came up to her and complimented her on her chic hairstyle—the blond buzz cut. It probably looked regal on her, because she was so tall and carried herself with such ease. And instead of saying "It's from chemo," she would smile and say thank you. Her tumors were frozen in place—not shrinking but not growing, either. As far as Lisa was concerned, she was in a holding pattern for a miracle that was sure to be on its way in the lab of some chemist or geneticist or oncologist, and like this woman in the white turban, the wait hadn't diminished her sense of hope.

I was placed in a twelve-week newly diagnosed breast cancer group the following week. There were about twelve women in the room. Four of them were under forty. Three of those had small children, like me. All but two were much further along in their treatment than I was. As we went around the room and told our stories, I felt like a soldier must feel who's been drafted but who has not yet seen battle. These women were warriors who had been through everything—mastectomy, double mastectomy, chemo, radiation, the works. They were stripped of everything from their hair to their health, and they were determined to be well.

When it came my turn to tell about my cancer, I felt like apologizing—for not wanting to join them, for not having a cancer that had gone beyond the breast, for not having been through chemo. Instead I just explained what Dr. Peter had told me about having to lose my breast, said that I was terrified, and hoped that I could somehow be as strong as they were.

I left the group that night realizing how much wider the gap was between the heroic TV-insurance-ad dad and my own dad: there was so little any of us could do in the face of this disease, besides share stories and fold underwear.

Lesson #6

The Victoria's Secret Catalog
Never Stops Coming

You can't ignore the images of beautiful breasts that pervade our society and you can't stop your own breast from being damaged. What you can do, however, is make sure you mourn the loss.

In the weeks before my mastectomy, in the long pre-Christmas season, the Victoria's Secret catalog never stopped coming. There was some sort of glitch in the mail system—or some special preholiday blitz—and I got two or three catalogs in the course of a few weeks, always on a day that I learned that something more—and worse—was going to happen to my breast. There I was, agonizing over the damage about to be done to me, and there they were—all those bare bodies, all those beautiful, smooth, and perfectly balanced breasts, all those pretty pieces of underwear designed to show them off.

It's easy enough to cancel a catalog—at least in theory. But if it wasn't the Victoria's Secret catalog coming in the mailbox, it was their models featured in the *Sports Illustrated* swimsuit issue, Tyra Banks in a tiny red bikini on the cover of GQ, or the now-famous Victoria's Secret Web site ad in the middle of the Super Bowl. Idealized breasts were everywhere I turned and I couldn't help but stare.

I tried to make myself go back to the stacks of breast cancer guidebooks to look at the unlit and unposed photos of women before and after their surgeries, but now that the question of mastectomy wasn't philosophical, I didn't want to see those pictures. The women they featured were not beautiful. They had cellulite on their tummies and fat on their arms, thin little rib cages and fleshy middles with angry red scars snaking across the skin. They had pendulous breasts and little pointy breasts, huge-nippled breasts and dimpled breasts, breasts that were dented and cut and mashed and removed. Every one of the pictures made me turn my head as if I had been slapped.

"You're going about this all wrong," Lori insisted on one of the many afternoons she sat with me at my kitchen table so I wouldn't have to sit there alone. "These are hilarious. Look at this one," she said, pointing to a woman with droopy breasts. "She probably breast-fed about ten kids. And this one?" she said, picking out a woman with large dark circles around her nipples. "Perfect for target practice." I couldn't help but laugh at

Lori's loopy sense of humor and was filled with gratitude for her willingness to say anything that had to be said.

"What's so funny?" Carlyn asked, suddenly appearing at my side.

"Nothing," I said, snapping the book shut.

"What?" she pressed.

"It's none of your business," Lori said.

This, of course, drew the whole crowd of kids in the house—Carlyn and Emily and Lori's kids, Kimber and Sarah. "We want to see! We want to see!" they chanted.

"No way!" we chanted back. We owned those pages now, and we needed them. One of those surgeries was going to be the one I picked.

∽

A few nights later Rob and I were back in the backyard hot tub.

"So do you think I should get breasts like Tyra's?" I asked—because what was I going to say: Will you still love me when I lose my breast? Will you still touch me? It's dark out there in the warm water, and you can say almost anything that has to be said—but there are some things even the darkness can't hold.

"They're nice on her, but on you? I don't think so," he said.

"You mean you wouldn't like it?"

"Sure I'd like it, but that's not why we have great sex," he said.

"They're kind of a critical component," I countered.

He shook his head. "I don't think so. I mean, what's great when we have great sex?"

"Your smell, the mood, what you do," I blurted.

"Not breasts," he said, like a lawyer making a closing argument.

"That's easy for you to say—and it's also not what you said before this was a reality."

"That's not fair," Rob snapped.

The breeze blew; the fog rolled in over our heads.

After a moment, he asked, "What makes it hard for you?"

I took a breath and cataloged the things about my breast that I would miss: the sensation of having my kids lean up against me when we read books at night; the feeling of pressing against another person when I give them a hug; the pride I have that these breasts did a good job at what they were intended to do; the warm and comforting feeling of Rob's hands on them; the way the nipples respond to his touch; the exact shape, weight, and balance of them; the fact that they are mine. I stopped to breathe. Rob sat unmoving across from me—frozen as if we were sitting in ice.

"I never thought about half those things," Rob said quietly.

I looked out at the night, dry-eyed and grief-stricken.

"We don't need your breast," he said. "We'll get used to it."

He moved behind me and cupped his hands around

me the way I like. It could have been any night, but it was one of our last nights, and all I could think about was what it would feel like not to feel that feeling and what it would be like to thumb through the Victoria's Secret catalog, the next time it came, with longing for what I'd lost rather than envy for what I'd never had.

Lesson #7

Magic Happens

If you've got to have breast cancer, it's a good time in history to have it. It used to be that a woman got a diagnosis of breast cancer and the next day—no questions asked, no discussion waged—she had a mastectomy. Before that, no one even knew what the problem was until the patient was dead. We may not have a cure for cancer—yet—but we've got sophisticated diagnostic tools, skilled physicians, and some pretty amazing ways to treat this disease.

I wanted to hate Dr. Black. The procedure that he performed—taking tissue from the tummy to build a new breast—was not only frighteningly invasive, it was suspicious in the way that cloning or genetic testing is: so advanced as to be morally questionable. I had no idea how to make a good decision about the surgical choices I had for my mastectomy and breast reconstruction, and labeling something—or someone—as suspect seemed as reasonable a way as any to narrow the field of options.

The degree to which breast cancer patients are left to make their own decisions is staggering. I expected that I might be assigned some sort of guide—someone to walk me through all the steps and stages of diagnosis and treatment, someone to tell me how to proceed and weigh all the choices I had before me. I expected a den mother. What I got instead was nothing—or rather no one. Everyone who was involved in my care was a specialist in his or her field and had an acute sense of where their expertise began and where it left off, but none of them had a big-picture view of my cancer. The long list of printed questions I took into each doctor's visit was never entirely answered by any one doctor. There was always a point at which the oncologist said to speak to the breast surgeon or the breast surgeon said to speak to the plastic surgeon. Couldn't all these people be persuaded to meet? Sit around a conference table, drink coffee, and discuss all the options? There were, after all, so many options.

I knew I had to have a mastectomy—a modified radical mastectomy. That was a given, due to the dirty margins on the tissue taken during my lumpectomy. One night during the long Thanksgiving weekend, in a fit of desperation, Rob had me take out a piece of paper and simply write those words down in a column with the heading Known Facts. Known fact: I have to have a mastectomy. From there, however, there seemed an endless number of roads to take.

I could, for instance, have the mastectomy and do nothing else. A woman from church—a small woman twice my age, with a British accent and a crooked front tooth—had taken me into the bathroom one Sunday after the service, unbuttoned her cream-colored blouse, removed her lacy bra and prostheses, and shown me her double mastectomy scars. Her chest was flat and rippled, like a washboard. It looked hard and healthy and somehow natural. This appealed to me—doing only what had to be done and living with the consequences. It had a certain stoicism to it and made a certain statement. But she was a seventy-year-old grandmother. I was thirty-five, and I wanted my body to be as close to what it would have been if I'd never gotten cancer. I wanted it to be round and full and balanced.

I could have a mastectomy and rebuild my breast with a saline or silicone implant. I'd heard that some doctors give you a basket filled with the various models. You pick through them and choose the one you like best. The doctor I went to for a second opinion preferred anatomically shaped silicone. He led me into an examining room and sent in an office assistant after me. She was, the doctor informed me, a former cancer patient, and she'd had a double mastectomy. She came into the room and I saw immediately that she was even younger than I was. She wasted no time in whipping off her white T-shirt to reveal a pair of rebuilt breasts that looked as firm and symmetrical as Barbie's, with unnaturally red and round nipples, which she explained to me had been made from the skin of a cadaver. Before I knew it, the words escaped: "Can I touch them?" I had never in my life touched another woman's breasts, but at that moment, in that examining room, it seemed critical. The assistant shrugged her shoulders slightly and nodded her assent. I had the thought that this must be part of her job description here at the oncologist's office: show patients your breasts on command and say yes if they ask to touch them.

I reached out and poked her right breast with my pointer finger as if I was testing a cantaloupe at the grocery store. It was very firm—like rubber—and slightly cooler than I thought it should be. I recoiled. I didn't like the idea of putting something so alien in my body. I smiled, thanked the assistant, and turned my head while she put her shirt back on.

The other option for reconstruction was the procedure performed by Dr. Black, known as the TRAM (transverse rectus abdominis myocutaneous) flap, or the free-flap. There were exactly eight plastic surgeons in the entire Los Angeles metropolitan area who could do the free-flap, and Dr. Black was one of them—the one unanimously recommended by my breast surgeon, my oncologist, my family practitioner, and two of the women in my support group.

I had to have a mastectomy—it was written right there in black and white in the Known Facts column. A mastectomy alone, though dramatic, is a relatively simple procedure. Adding implants adds a little time, and at least a second surgery. The free-flap surgery, however, turns the reconstructive process from a day trip into an extended world tour.

My plan was that I would meet Dr. Black, hate him and his complicated surgery, and be forced into accepting one of the other options. I'd heard from other doctors that Dr. Black was young and so eager to do his magic operation that he wouldn't even discuss the idea of implants with patients. I'd heard from other women that he was arrogant. I was sure it would be easy to hate him.

His office was equidistant between the two hospitals in our area. It wasn't in one of the fancy glass office buildings that surround the hospitals; it was off on its own, on a busy thoroughfare, next to a chiropractor's office.

Rob and I walked into the waiting room and I bristled. The magazines were spread out on the floor because there was no coffee table. There were no pictures on the walls, no plants, no goldfish, no stacks of cheerful pamphlets. It was an attractive room, with a curved, shoulder-high receptionist's desk and a soaring ceiling, but all I could see was what wasn't there. I sat stiffly, looking at back issues of *Time*, until an assistant called us to follow her to an examination room. As we walked down the hallway, she informed us that they had just moved into this space. The painters, in fact, had only been out a few days. I nodded, feeling marginally better about the lack of pamphlets.

The examining room was carpeted. Rob seated himself on a pretty, straight-backed chair. I climbed up and sat on the end of the small examining table. My legs dangled off the end, like those of a little girl sitting on the end of a dock on a lake on a sunny day. There were no diplomas on the walls and no instruments on the shelves. There was a cheap wardrobe mirror leaning against the wall.

"Strange," I whispered to Rob.

"It's like he just hung out his shingle," Rob replied.

"I guess we'll see," I said, shrugging my shoulders and going back to *Time*, as if there was nothing to discuss and nothing to do but wait until this doctor came in to prove himself.

We heard Dr. Black before we saw him. He was on the phone. He was arguing with someone about how he couldn't possibly take on a particular case because there was no doctor in the area qualified enough to assist him and he needed such a doctor to do the job. Rob looked at me and raised his eyebrows as if to say, See? Conceited. I shook my head and pressed my lips together into a knowing grin. Suddenly Dr. Black knocked on the door and came in. He wore a denim work shirt, wrinkled, with the sleeves rolled up. He wore a pair of work boots that looked as if they'd slogged through a horse corral. His dirty blond hair hung in soft curves below his ears and across his forehead. He looked like a surfer or a rock star. There was no white coat, no stethoscope. His eyes were very blue and unwavering. I kept waiting for him to say, "I'm one of the painters; Dr. Black will be here in a moment"—but he never did.

"How can I help you?" he asked.

"I'm not sure you can," I said.

"I'm so sorry to hear about your cancer," Dr. Black continued. "It's a terrible thing."

"Yes," I said, trying to twist his words so they didn't sound so compassionate.

"I heard about your case at the tumor board," he said. "At least I think it was you." I noticed at this point that he had no chart, no pad of paper, no doctor tools of any kind. He had no idea who I was. "It was a lumpectomy with Dr. Peter, about here," he said, reaching out a thick, scrubbed finger and pointing at my breast, "with dirty margins. It's very sad that you have to lose your breast for a cancer you caught so early."

I nodded. He'd gotten my story exactly right.

"What I do is the Cadillac of reconstructions," he said, as if in answer to a question. "It's state of the art." Dr. Black was giving us a lecture, not a sales pitch, and just as though we were students in a lecture hall, Rob sat back, crossed his legs, and cocked his head to listen. I crossed my arms, the more reluctant student, saying with my body, "Prove to me you have anything worthwhile to say."

"The idea originated with the tummy tuck surgery," Dr. Black began. He asked me to get off the examining table, so I climbed off and leaned against the wall next to Rob. Using a black Sharpie pen he pulled from his pocket, Dr. Black proceeded to draw the outline of a very shapely woman on the white tissue paper that was stretched across the table. He drew in the breasts and he drew in the belly button. Next he drew a large ellipse around the belly button, extending from hip to hip. It looked like an elongated football. "All this tissue was being taken out and thrown away, until someone came up with the idea of using it to rebuild a woman's own breast." He walked over to the counter, opened an apothecary tin, pulled out a pair of long scissors, came back, and began to cut the football out of his drawing. He explained how the traditional TRAM flap took the tummy tissue, pushed it up inside the chest, and, with the blood vessels still connected, built a new breast. He demonstrated this scenario by cutting out a strip of paper that reached from the top of the football to the collarbone. He folded this like an accordion, pulling the football up to the breast. As he held the paper in place, he explained the limitations of this operation— the fact that the blood had to travel down to the tummy and back up to the breast, the inability to avoid a bump in the middle of the chest, the incredibly invasive nature of the surgery to tunnel through the entire abdomen.

Rob and I stared at the paper woman, waiting for the payoff we knew was coming. "What I do," Dr. Black continued, "is called a free-flap." He snipped the ellipse free of its tether and placed it neatly over the breast. "I remove the skin and tissue from the tummy and reconnect the blood vessels right at the site. It's a beautiful result. Nothing else is like it."

There was a moment of silence as this extraordinary description hung in the air among us.

"Don't you have a philosophical problem cutting

women up and moving their body parts around?" I blurted into the quiet.

Dr. Black smiled. "Do you have any kids?"

"Two girls," I said.

"Suppose one of them lost her finger. Would you let me sew it back on?"

"Of course," I said.

"What if she lost her thumb and it couldn't be reattached. Would you let me connect one of her toes so she could have an opposable thumb?"

"Yes," I said. Then more quietly, "It's amazing you can do that."

"This is no different," he explained. "You're going to lose your breast. I can make you a new one."

"But a breast is different from a thumb," I argued, thinking about Lisa and her damaged lungs, which she could feel failing with every single constricted breath she took and for which there was, in her case, no replacement, and without which she wasn't going to live to help her children if they ever lost a finger under the whirring blade of a table saw or even just dented one in the door of a car. "You don't really *need* a breast."

"I can't make that decision for you," he said.

Ah ha! I thought. And why not? Why can't you make that decision for me? Why can't anyone? Why isn't there someone in this roster of high-priced doctors who can tell me what to do?

"It's a huge surgery," I went on, repeating words I'd heard other people use.

"I'm not going to kid you, it's a long surgery," Dr. Black answered, "and the recovery is long—about two months. But when you're thirty-five, two months isn't much measured against the rest of your life."

I began to wonder if Dr. Black was yet thirty-five. I tried to remember from friends' stories how long it took to get through med school, residencies, and internships.

As if he could read my thoughts, Rob began to grill Dr. Black about his credentials—why wasn't he affiliated with a major medical center, where had he trained, what were his success ratios. Dr. Black calmly answered each question with perfect honesty, integrity, and an alarmingly accomplished string of experiences. At the end of the exchange, Rob asked why we didn't need to do this big surgery at a big hospital. "There are eight surgeons in Los Angeles who do this surgery," Dr. Black answered, "and we can do it anywhere we want. All I need is eight hours and a microscope at one of the hospitals where I have privileges."

Rob was, by this point, rendered speechless.

"But I'm terrified," I said, resorting to the last argument in my arsenal. "I'd like to speak to one of your patients who's had the surgery." I wanted some living, breathing assurance that the surgery worked, that people survived it, and that it wasn't just sleight-of-hand and mirrors.

Dr. Black shook his head, apologized, and said this simply couldn't be done.

"But I'm terrified," I repeated. "I want to talk to someone who's been through it."

"I'm sorry," he said, shrugging his shoulders. There was no sales pitch, even now.

We shook his hand and said we'd get back to him, but I didn't think we would. When we got into the car, I told Rob I didn't like the boots and I didn't like the shirt and I didn't like the fact that I couldn't talk to a patient. Rob nodded and said he was impressed by the drawing, impressed by the credentials, and impressed by the compassion.

I went to sleep more confused than ever.

The next day, around dinnertime, a woman called me from the cell phone in her car. She said her name was Lori Molina and that she was a patient of Dr. Black's. She sounded like she was about my age, and she shared the first name of one of my best friends. She told me that she'd had the free-flap a year ago and that she could recommend Dr. Black to me without reservation. She also invited me to come see her breast. I took down her address and arranged to meet her at her apartment the following evening.

The next night Rob drove me across town to see the breast of a woman I'd never met. He parked the car at the curb and sat there while I went and knocked on the apartment door. We were two blocks from the beach and I could hear the waves crashing. "Hi. I'm Jennie," I said when Lori answered, "and this is the weirdest thing I've ever done." I didn't mention that having the assistant whip off her T-shirt in the other doctor's office was, in fact, weirder.

Lori was a tall woman with tightly curled red hair and

porcelain skin. She stood very tall, as if she were an Amazon queen, and I noticed immediately that the breasts beneath her loose blouse were large. She invited me in and led me across the apartment. It looked like a first apartment, with bookshelves made out of brick and planks, sagging couches, and a tiny galley kitchen, but she probably felt very lucky about it because it was only half a block from the beach. When we paraded in front of Lori's husband, who sat hunched down on the couch watching television, he nodded and said, "Hey." I smiled without opening my lips, wondering what he could possibly be thinking.

As soon as we got into the bedroom, Lori began to unbutton her blouse. She unhooked her bra in the front and exposed her breasts. They were enormous, round, perfectly matched and perfectly balanced breasts, and they were right there, a foot in front of me. They glowed with the same porcelain color as Lori's face and seemed to defy gravity the way they hung in the air. The rebuilt one looked as warm and real as the one on the other side. If it weren't for the round patch of skin right on the top of the breast, and the three black stitches alongside the nipple, you wouldn't know that it was a mound of totally numb tummy tissue, magically transformed into a breast. At first, I pretended to be very clinical—oh, yes, I see the stitches there on your nipple, and, yes, I see what he means about the scar extending up under the arm—but I was amazed by the beautiful shape of her breast. It was hard not to gape.

"Dr. Black just made the nipple a few weeks ago," Lori explained, "but a few of the stitches popped out. That's why I was in to see him yesterday. He told me he had a patient about my age who was scared and I offered to call."

"Did that hurt?" I asked. "The nipple? The stitches?" The stitches were made of large black thread, weaving in and out of raw red skin.

She shook her head and tweaked her new nipple. "It's numb. The whole breast is numb. He didn't even use anesthesia."

I swallowed. "But what about the surgery? Did it hurt?"

"It was rough, but it was nothing next to chemo," she said. "And you get over it in time." Next she unbuckled her pants and showed me her hip-to-hip scar, where the outline of the football was sewn together. Already, the line was faded to the white of her skin. Already, the flesh from her tummy was at home somewhere else on her body.

I looked back at her breast. "Would you mind if I touched it?" I asked—for the second time in two weeks.

"Not at all," Lori said.

I reached out a finger and felt warm, yielding flesh. "You can't feel that?" I asked, dropping my hand.

"I know someone's touching me, but that's about it," she said.

As she buttoned her blouse and zipped her pants, she told me about how she discovered her cancer six months before she was to be married, and how she went ahead with the wedding even though her hair was still growing in from the chemo. She showed me a picture of herself with her fiancé. Her red hair hung in ringlets to her waist. "My hair was my trademark," she said wistfully. "I hope it grows back quickly."

"I like it short, for what it's worth. It's cute." It was, in fact, stunning—a small crown of deep red ringlets.

She ran her hand through her curls and frowned. "I'm also hoping my period will come back," she said. "There's nothing I want in the world more than children."

I felt my terror shrink to the size of a pea. I didn't even need to ask for reassurance from this fearless woman; I just needed to stand in her presence and feed off her courage. She was well and she was whole, and so, one day, would I be.

"I hope so, too," I said.

As I stopped at the door to say good-bye, Lori's husband grunted at me again. "One thing," he said, and I braced myself for him to say something strange. "Just remember that when the dark days come, let them come." He nodded at his own sage advice. I felt like crossing the room to hug him.

"I'll try," I said. "Thank you." I thought of Rob waiting for me in the car and what he must be going through— the terror of having a wife with cancer and the sadness of being excluded from what was going on in that apartment. "Your wife is beautiful," I added, and I walked out the door.

The next week I went back to see Dr. Black. When he walked into the examining room—wearing a short-sleeved piqué polo shirt and a pair of khakis—he smiled and said, "You changed your mind."

I had indeed. Lori's breast had convinced me. My breast wouldn't be anywhere near as spectacular as hers, but it would be warm and natural. It would always be numb but alive enough to gain and lose weight as the rest of me would, and age and sag as the rest of me might. It would be as much mine as the original one had been— perhaps for an even longer period of time—and all this for one day of surgery and two months of recovery and a nipple-making process I wouldn't even feel.

"I think what you do is magic," I said.

Dr. Black considered this for a millisecond, shrugged his shoulders, and said, "I think you're right."

Lesson #8

Caregivers Are Human

When you're in the middle of cancer treatment, you're not in control. Chemo patients talk about not knowing how their body is going to behave from one minute to the next, which is a pretty good description of the whole cancer experience. Every doctor is different, every drug is different, and every day is different. The same can be said about husbands and mothers, friends and neighbors. They're not necessarily going to behave how you want them to behave or how they usually behave or how you need them to behave— and there's not a thing you can do about it. They do what they can, and you do what you can to recover.

In the weeks leading up to my surgery, fear and anxiety ruled my days and nights and drove me to obsess about how my household would function in my absence. I was scheduled to be in the hospital for five to seven days, but part of me was orchestrating a world in which I was no longer a useful part. Part of me was planning as if I might never come back.

It was the season of school Christmas parties and special events, and I couldn't see how any one person could keep track of everything that was happening—not even Rob, and particularly not if he was the one who would be in charge of my care while I was unable to care for myself. To ease my anxiety, I created a Master Plan that listed the events of the coming days in excruciating detail and recruited friends and family to fill in all the blanks. My mom would walk the kids to school, pick them up, and take them to see *Stuart Little* when it came out. My friend Carol would coordinate the meals that were offered from people at church, and Denise would coordinate the meals that were offered from people in the neighborhood. Lori was on call if Carlyn or Emily needed somewhere to go for a few hours or a few days, and she was also my backup in case one of my clients fell into a panic over a headline or a chapter summary—an unlikely event, given the fact that I had already met all my deadlines for December as well as January. My sister, my dad, and Honeydew were poised to help when I came home from the hospital, when, I suspected, the rest of us would be exhausted.

Manic planning, ironically, does little to ease the anxiety that inspires it. I had everything organized and written out, but I still couldn't sleep at night. I'd get up and write Christmas cards and wrap presents—thinking, again, that if I died during the surgery, at least everyone I knew would have one last thing to remember me by. When there were no more cards to write, I lay in bed and listened to a guided imagery tape. A woman with a rich and liquid voice led me step-by-step through the events leading up to surgery. "You are awake on the table, but sleepy. The lights are very bright. Hear the sounds of the doctors and nurses as they go about preparing to do the work they have trained to do," the tape urged. I clung to these images and words as if they could reduce my terror, as if they would give me some modicum of control in a situation where, by design, I would have none. The last command on the tape was to picture my family and loved ones holding hands in a circle around me. It was to be a circle of love, peace, and healing. In my visualizations, I always pictured them around a campfire, but in reality, they didn't form a circle. They were more like a parade of people just doing what they could to keep smiling as they got nearer and nearer to the end of the route.

The first person to come help was my friend Bridget. She flew in from Philadelphia two days before my surgery, leaving her husband and two kids behind. "I can't not come," she'd told me several weeks before. "I'll do anything you need me to. I just need to be there." I knew what she meant: our concern for each other is so deep that it would be impossible just to stand by during a difficult time. I'd lived with Bridget—through many small

and large difficulties—for longer than I'd lived with anyone except my family. We were randomly assigned to be
freshman roommates in college, and we elected to be
roommates every year thereafter until, two years after
we earned our degrees, Bridget got married.

She came to · California for my mastectomy and
changed the whole feeling in our home. She brought a
sense of calm we hadn't felt in months. She took the girls
out for hamburgers one night so Rob and I could be alone
together in a house that was quiet. She gave me an
antique bell inscribed with the faded red words *Enjoy
yourself,* so I could call for help from my bed. The night
before the surgery, she took us all to Benihana, where we
had grilled scallops and sweet drinks with paper umbrella
ornaments. Before we went to sleep that night, she took a
picture of me and Rob—a snapshot that frames our
weary, anxious, and frightened faces.

On the morning of my surgery, I wasn't supposed to
eat breakfast. I busied myself making the girls' lunches,
tying their shoes, and telling them—one more time—that
my mom was going to pick them up from school for the
remainder of the week. I'd made them draw pictures of
me in the hospital being taken care of by a smiling nurse
and a smiling doctor because I'd read somewhere that
this can reduce anxiety. They dutifully drew the scene,
and I suppose it worked, because all they wanted were
the most basic reassurances: would I miss them and when
was I coming home? I felt an overwhelming gratefulness
for how simple and self-centered their lives were. They

were so easy to please and so easy to love. All you had to do was want to be with them and that was more than enough. I dropped them off at their respective schools with nothing more than their regular hugs, and they disappeared into the sea of children as if it were an ordinary day.

My mom arrived at our house, her arms full of food and gifts, her manner light and cheerful. It seemed as though, on the two-hour drive from Santa Barbara, she had steeled herself to be upbeat. She laughed when I thrust my lists and schedules at her and showed her where the M&M's for Carlyn's class cookie decorating party were hidden, but as the breadth and depth of my planning became clear to her, her smile began to fade. By the time Bridget, Rob, and I got in the car to drive to the hospital, nothing could mask her worry.

"Good luck," she croaked, as she stood on the front lawn, waving good-bye.

"Don't forget to leave the light on for Emily!" I yelled back, as Rob pulled away from the curb.

In the pre-op room at the hospital, I stood and let Dr. Black draw with a black Sharpie pen all over my body where he was going to cut—lines and dashes and a large X to the left of my belly button where the skin for my new breast would come from. "Wow," Rob said when he saw the guidelines. He peered at them and tried to understand what each of them meant. Bridget, by contrast, turned gray and began to cry. It was this—her face—that made my own eyes fill with tears and made me say, strangely, "I don't know why I'm crying." Dr. Peter, who would be doing the mastectomy before Dr. Black did the reconstruction, walked around the side of my bed and wordlessly wiped the tears that spilled from my eyes. Bridget put her hand over her mouth the way you do when something is unspeakable.

When the anesthesiologist started the IV drip, I told Rob that I loved him. I don't remember being wheeled away from him, but I have a vague memory of the bright lights and bustle in the operating room—just as I'd been told to picture in my visualization tape.

∽

After a free-flap surgery, you spend twenty-four hours in the ICU so that the nurses can check for the blood flow in the repositioned tummy flesh. They come in every hour with a little Doppler machine like the one used for listening to the heartbeats of babies in utero. During my first night in critical care, Bridget was there. She later told me that she thought I looked dead, lying so pale and still. I don't remember anything about her time there except her presence and a few licks of cold washcloth on my head. It felt so good—both because she seemed to know just what to do and because her presence was so uncomplicated.

Rob came next. He held my hand. That's what I remember—that and the more complex nature of his worry. I could feel it, or smell it, or sense it. He wanted me to be back to the way I was. He wanted this to be over. He'd not only lived through his mother's death, six years before, he'd also watched his dad kill himself, three weeks before his mom died, with a final, furious binge of scotch. After all that, and now all this, Rob could barely contain his worry and his love. I wanted him near me because the very fact of my breath and my heartbeat brought him comfort, as his did me, but his concern felt heavy.

My mom was there, later, rubbing my feet. She was concerned and unsure—unsure of how to help me, unsure of what to do with Rob's worry, unsure of what to do with the fact that she couldn't save this day as she had saved so many others, by sheer force of organization and perseverance. My mom doesn't like sickness, let alone hospitals and blood. As children, my sister and I came to believe that she didn't allow it. I once worked with a woman who revealed to me that when she was a child, she used to feign illness so she could stay home from school to be with her mother. She would do all those things you hear about in the movies—run a thermometer under hot tap water and wet the sheets to mimic a sweat—and it worked. What I loved most about the story wasn't just the fact of my friend getting away with murder; I loved the fact of her mother's indulgence because I had a far more practical mother than that. My mom always just seemed to will me to be well, and I always followed her command—until now.

I ended up staying in the ICU for two extra days

because I couldn't stop throwing up. My peculiar reaction to narcotics extends to the antinausea drugs they give you to stop the convulsions; they don't seem to work for me. I curled up into the tightest ball I could manage and willed myself not to retch. It didn't work. I heaved and heaved, though there was nothing in my system to come up. During all this heaving, something in my abdomen popped— a stitch or a tuck—and I started to bleed internally. I developed a fever that spiked. My blood pressure plunged and I required first one, then another unit of blood. My situation was suddenly precarious.

As if they were a mirror of my state of health, my caretaking team fell apart, too. Bridget had to return to Philadelphia, and my mother and Rob got into a fight. They each wanted to be in control—of me, of my body, of each other—and neither of them had a chance of succeeding.

"If she can't communicate, she's got to go home," Rob declared.

"If he's going to give ultimatums, I can't stay here," my mom railed.

They'd never before clashed about anything more important than what the girls could or could not eat for dinner, and now, as I lay in a bed in a critical care unit of a hospital, bleeding into my belly, their fury at each other grew so strong they couldn't even sleep in the same house.

I wanted to yell, "Stop it! Both of you!" as if I were the mother and they were the kids. I wanted to page Bridget at the airport and beg her to return with her single suit-case and her simple love. I wanted my mother to lighten up and my husband to calm down and my body to heal so that so much concern wasn't necessary, but I had no power over any of it. I was reminded of a woman in my support group who was so weak from chemo, she couldn't even make it back from the bathroom to the bedroom and fell asleep in the hall. This was in her mother's house, where she was staying while she was sick. She awoke to hear her grandmother asking her mother when she was going to stop throwing up and go home. She listened to the conversation, felt its sharp sting, then bent her head and fell back asleep.

✑

On my third day in the ICU, Rob brought Carlyn and Emily to visit. They brought construction-paper cards they had made for me, filled with Christmas stickers and hand-drawn hearts. They played with the controls on my bed, making me go up and down within an arc of about ten degrees. I asked them, as cheerfully as I could, how school was going and how it was having so many visitors at the house, and what they'd been eating for dinner, but I was desperate for them to leave. I felt as if I might throw up at any moment and I didn't want them to be there. I suggested they go up to the maternity floor to see the babies. Rob took my cue, and within minutes they were gone.

After four days, my condition was more stable and I was moved out of the ICU up to the regular recovery floor. It seemed, suddenly, as if I was terribly alone. Rob was watching the girls now that they were out of school for the holidays, my mom had returned to Santa Barbara, and my dad and Honeydew had yet to arrive on their boat. Friends came to visit me—Lori Logan and Jo—but there was no one keeping vigil by my side. There was another woman in the room with me who'd had an emergency hysterectomy. A thin curtain separated us, and I hardly even knew she was there. One night, in the middle of the night, a very young nurse came in to take my blood. She kept missing the vein, trying again, and missing the vein. "Please," I begged her, making my first, monumentally difficult effort at changing the course of my own recovery, "can you please go get someone who can do this on the first try." The nurse scurried out, and I began to sob—with terror at how fragile I was and anger that no one was there at that particular moment, in the dark of the night, to speak on my behalf.

"You're going to be okay," said the woman on the other side of the curtain. It sounded, somehow, as if God had decided to speak.

"I don't know," I replied to the darkness. "I can't take it anymore." I meant being ill, being needy, being loved so much, and being loved in the imperfect way that humans do.

"You've been through a lot. It will get better. She's going to bring a nurse who can do it right."

"Thank you," I mumbled, licking the salty tears that slid down my face.

⁊

I did get better. I managed to go pee on my own. I hobbled to the shower in the hallway, unpinned the four drains pinned to my hospital gown, sat on a plastic bench, and let Rob wash my hair. I made my way to the nurses' station, step by agonizing step, with a pillow pressed to my tummy, bent over nearly forty-five degrees, to prove to my dad and Honeydew that I was okay. When the pharmacist came to try to help find a better mix of painkillers and he turned out to be a tall, handsome man, Honeydew and I joked about calling him back for more consultations.

At the end of my week in the hospital, Dr. Black came striding into my room, late in the evening, wearing very rumpled green scrubs and carrying a folder that was an inch and a half thick. It had my name on the tab. "We got clean margins," he said, "and clean lymph nodes. And do you know that there was cancer all over that breast? Everywhere. We did exactly the right thing, doing this mastectomy. This is an amazing pathology report and you're a very, very lucky woman." Since all the breast tissue was gone, I wouldn't have to have radiation. Since the lymph nodes and margins were clean, I wouldn't have to have chemotherapy.

I felt the cool rush of relief, a knot of giddiness in my stomach, and gratefulness as bright as the sun. But I also felt a sense of doubt—a shadow of the danger that had been so close. It could so easily have gone the other way. Dr. Black could so easily have been standing there, bedraggled and tired, saying, "I'm sorry." There was no reason, besides luck, that it had gone the way it did. "Wow," I whispered.

I called my mom and my sister to tell them the good news and rode home under the watch of a huge moon. It was the biggest moon in 365 years, my dad told me, because of an unusual coincidence in the alignment of the moon and the earth. Our house seemed to be glowing and someone had placed a candle on a bucket at the curb to herald my arrival. Carlyn and Emily ran out of the house in their pajamas to greet me, jumping up and down outside the car door. When I saw them, I burst into tears. I had forgotten them, in the last week, for more hours than I had ever forgotten them in the course of their entire lives.

"They're so beautiful," I cried.

Rob cried, too—the first time he had since I'd been diagnosed. "Aren't they?" he agreed as tears streamed down his face.

When I got inside, I sat on the couch while the girls plastered more stickers on my slippers—dogs and cats and angels and Christmas trees—and I trembled with fear that they might jump onto my lap or lean on my breast. When my dad insisted, the next night, that we take a drive to see the enormous moon rise over the city and celebrate our place on the earth, I held my breath in fear that we would hit a pothole or a speed bump. I felt as if I'd already used up all my luck, and the world seemed like a dangerous place.

❧

My mom came back three days after I came home, with steely determination to continue to be of use by cooking us Christmas dinner. While Carlyn and Emily played with their new toys, she cooked an elaborate meal of roast beef and popovers, stewed beets, and parsnip puree. I watched her from the couch as if I were watching a performance. My ninety-year-old grandma, who had come with my mom for the day, sat beside me and kept asking why I didn't seem like myself. I tried explaining that I had just had major surgery, but this didn't seem to sink in. "It's cancer, Grandma," I finally shouted. "I had cancer." Satisfied, she took another tack: "Why is your mother working so hard in the kitchen?" My mom was cooking because she was the mom, because she loved me and was grateful I wasn't going to die. She was cooking because cooking was what she could do. "She's working so hard because it's Christmas," I said.

My mom and Rob spoke to each other only as necessary, with cool civility. When dinner was over, she wrapped up the mountains of leftovers to feed us for the rest of the week, did the dishes, and drove my grandmother home. There was never any question whether or not my mom was going to spend the night under the same roof as Rob.

My sister, Laura—older than me by three years and more unflappable by a number of degrees—flew out from Connecticut with her two daughters the next day. Because of the schedule at the university where she was a professor of music, it was the earliest she'd been able to come. She worried that she was arriving too late in my recovery to be of any help, and even though I assured her that I was relieved and grateful she had come, she bent over backward to be of use. I sat on my spot on the couch and watched her feed three meals a day to all four kids, organize trips to the park, to the movies, and to the zoo, and vacuum the carpets in between. In one afternoon, Laura stripped the Christmas tree, boxed up all the ornaments, wrapped up all the lights, and dragged the tree to the curb for recycling.

It was during Laura's visit that I felt like I began to heal. The pain across my belly began to subside and, with it, my need for narcotics. Laura also soothed the pain of the rift between my mother and Rob by telling me not to worry, that everything would resolve itself with time, that the important thing was for me to get healthy and strong. I was finally able to relax and to sleep.

Carlyn and Emily, on the other hand, grew tired of so many visitors and so much activity. It had been a long three weeks for them.

"I want to do something just with you," Carlyn begged.

"I'll be back to normal soon," I promised.

"When?" she wanted to know.

"By the time school starts again," I said.

"Will you be able to stand up straight by then?"

"Straighter," I said.

"And walk around?"

"A little," I said.

She nodded, and set her sights on the return to school.

∽

On New Year's Eve—the eve of the new millennium—my dad and Honeydew returned for a family feast, which Laura whipped up from all the leftovers in the refrigerator. We had just turned on the TV to watch the coverage from around the world, when my friend Doug called to see how I was doing. I shared with him the good news about my clean margins and described the place where I sat on the couch, surrounded by pillows and magazines, kids and cups of tea. I would have described to him the quirks of the feud between Rob and my mom—because he's known us all for such a long time and would have laughed and understood—but my dad and Honeydew were there and Rob was there and they were all doing what they could do to help. It didn't seem fair to speak of it.

"Lisa's home, too," Doug said.

My breath stopped on the inhale. "Home?"

"She was in the hospital," he explained, and when I said nothing, he said, "You didn't know?"

"No," I cried, feeling frantic. "What happened?"

"Her lungs filled with fluid. They rushed her to emergency and cut her open."

My eyes filled with tears. She hadn't been able to listen to guided imagery tapes. She hadn't been able to carefully arrange a long string of caregivers to sit by her side. She wasn't going to get a great piece of news at the end of her hospital stay—only the news that she could breathe again, at least for a little while, with her damaged and ravaged lungs. "Is she okay?" I asked, hoping stupidly that Doug could tell me that she was going to be fine.

"All I heard was that she's home," he said. I bit my lip. Had I not just lost a breast, had I not just come from the hospital, I would have known that Lisa had had this setback, I would have had some piece of information to add to what Doug was offering, and I could have done at least something small to bring Lisa some comfort.

I sent Lisa a card because I didn't want to call and have her ask me how I was feeling, how I was doing, how my surgery had been. I didn't want to have to tell her how happy I'd been to hear the news that cancer hadn't invaded my blood and my bones. All I said in the card was that I'd heard she'd been having a tough time and that I was thinking of her.

I got a card from her in the return mail. It was classic Lisa. It said, "All surgeries are hard, but I hear yours was particularly brutal." It also said, "The tests they did in the hospital showed that my tumors have grown."

⁓

After I spoke to Doug, I needed to breathe new air. Laura—who can't stand sitting still—said she'd take me for a drive, so we got in the car and wandered around town, looking at the shops closing and the people making last-minute purchases for long-planned parties. By chance, we drove down a street that took us right to the edge of the ocean. I hadn't even considered that sunset on the last night of the century would be an occasion to celebrate, but there were people lining the street as if for a parade, arrayed with picnic baskets, binoculars, and telephoto lenses. The low, thick clouds were on fire with orange and pink and the people stood there, rapt. We turned onto the street that runs along the beach just in time to see the sun dip below the horizon, huge and silent. There seemed no reason, after that, to stay up to watch the fireworks.

In the following days, Laura went home, Rob went back to work, and the girls went back to school. My dad and Honeydew insisted on staying so they could be with me for the appointment at which I expected Dr. Black to remove my abdominal drains and pronounce that I was doing better than expected, I would be recovered sooner than he hoped, I would be back to my normal life in no time flat. At that office visit, Dr. Black poked and prodded my abdomen, announced that it was full of old blood—a hematoma, it was called, which sounded to me like a bad bruise or a mild headache—and said he had no choice but to reopen my abdominal wound. Fine, I thought, imagining that he would open it, drain it, then stitch it neatly together with his invisible thread. But then he was scooping his gloved hand inside my tummy and pressing with his open hands on both sides of the wound to get the old blood out, and I dug my fingernails into Honeydew's hand and understood that it might not be fine at all. He sent me immediately to the wound clinic at the hospital, a part of the burn unit where unspeakable wounds are slowly and torturously healed.

As soon as I arrived, a nurse named Heather took a Polaroid picture of my wound. It was a gash as deep and wide as a Ping-Pong ball and three times as long. I never saw the wound itself. I couldn't look at it. For a full month, in fact, I showered sitting on a plastic chair with two washcloths laid across my lap so I wouldn't have to look. I only saw the picture because it was sitting on the top of my record chart one day when the folder was lying open. A wound like that can't be stitched closed; it has to heal from the inside out. It has to be packed with yards and yards of gauze, two times a day, to keep it clean. I couldn't walk more than a few feet without assistance and I couldn't drive, but for thirty-two straight days, I had to go to the wound clinic at the hospital so they could clean the gash with saline and Q-tips and long-nosed tweezers. During that month, I did little more than sit and sleep. Carlyn and Emily watched videos every afternoon and begged me, daily, to stand up and walk them to school. Despite my inactivity, I ruined an entire drawerful of underwear with all the blood that oozed from my wound, and wrecked pants, pajamas, sheets, and towels. Each night as Rob packed the wound, with gloved hands and held breath, I held a pillow over my face and cried, not only because he seemed to have such an endless reserve of love and patience to draw from, but because the task was so awful that I was sure I would never be able to do the same for him. Like my mom, I don't like blood and guts. I get nervous around hospitals.

"You'd do what you could," he said.

Sometimes Crying Is the Point

*Kids cry over everything. They cry if they can't find
their shoes, they cry if there's a crack in their burrito,
they cry if it's raining on the day they had their
heart set on going to the park. If you ask kids why
they're crying over something that seems small and
trivial, they'll tell you: because I'm sad—or mad or
hurt. Somewhere along the line from being a kid to
being an adult, we forget how to cry. We forget how
natural it is, how expressive it is, and how good it
feels. If ever there's a time to relearn the lessons of
crying, having cancer has got to be it.*

The one thing I dreaded after Dr. Black reopened the
wound in my stomach was throwing up, and as if my
dread decided to come gleefully knock on the door and
camp out on the welcome mat, I got the stomach flu.

I knew it was coming. Carlyn had been sick the night before. I was in no position to mother anyone, but instinct took over, and I tried to help. I got out of bed and shuffled around the house collecting towels and buckets while Rob held Carlyn's head over the toilet. I let Carlyn curl up next to me in bed while Rob mopped up the floor. My stomach felt queasy, but at first I attributed this to the common revulsion of being around someone else's vomit. It wasn't until the following evening, when Carlyn was happily asleep, that I started to feel that feeling of no return. I knew I would soon be throwing up and there was nothing I could do to stop it.

I started to cry. At first, they were just silent tears.

"What's wrong, honey?" Rob said, when he walked in the bedroom and saw me crying.

"I'm going to throw up," I said. He looked around frantically for a bucket.

"Not this instant," I said, "but I'm going to throw up. I know it."

"Then let's go to the hospital right now," he said. "We can take the girls next door, get you up there, and get some drugs before it's too late." He was talking about antinausea drugs. IV drips. Needles in the arm. He was assuming that someone with a five-inch gash in her stomach should not be throwing up unassisted.

I started to cry harder. My face contorted—eyes squeezed, mouth in a violent frown. "I don't want to take the girls next door. I don't want to go to the hospital." I sobbed. I pictured sitting in a waiting room having to wait.

I pictured someone trying to stick an IV into my arm, where every vein was already punctured and bruised. I pictured the tiny little pink peanut-shaped plastic cup they hold under your mouth when you throw up.

This made Rob mad. "You either go to the hospital and deal with it now or you stay home and throw up. Which is it going to be?"

Now my whole body got into the crying—my shoulders shook, my stomach lurched—and even this mild wrenching caused pain. "Don't be mean to me," I whispered.

"I'm not being mean, I'm trying to help you," he said.

"You're being mean."

"Jennie. You have two choices. Get sick and deal with it or go to the hospital and get drugs to stop it. Which are you going to do?"

I thought about this for a moment. "I don't want to do either," I said. I was crying so hard now, I had to hold my head in one hand and my stomach in the other. "I'm not going to the hospital. But if I start to throw up," I went on, "I'm going to kill myself. There's only so much a person can take."

"Fine," Rob said. "After everything we've just done to save you, you go right ahead and kill yourself." He climbed into bed, turned off the light, rolled away from me, and went to sleep.

My tears went back to the silent kind, the pooling-in-the-ears kind. I sat there feeling as sorry for myself as I can ever remember feeling. I let myself dream of being dead—of being without a body that was so fragile. I thought about being an angel, floating, clean and white and bloodless, and the thought was pleasing.

I must have fallen asleep, because when I awoke, it was 3 A.M. and I knew without a doubt that I was about to throw up. I went from asleep to I'm going to throw up in 0.6 seconds. I clamped my mouth shut and inhaled through my nose as I eased my legs to the side of the bed, rolled over on my side, pushed myself forward, and got out of bed. I grabbed a pillow, shuffled as fast as I could to the toilet, kneeled before it, pressed the pillow into my abdomen, and threw up.

When it was over, I slumped against the wall and wailed. I wailed the way a child wails when they feel they've been wronged. This was too much to bear.

Rob stumbled into the bathroom and sat across from me in the dark. "What can I do to help?" he asked, suddenly solicitous.

"Nothing," I said, and cried even harder. I sounded like a native woman in some sort of primal ritual, bawling at the moon or the gods or both. I could hear myself—this strange sound I was making, this mournful wailing, and I remember thinking, I hope the girls don't wake up, but I had no interest in stopping. Rob wanted to help me, to stop me from crying, but at the moment crying was the only thing that made sense.

I stayed there for about fifteen minutes, face toward the sky, back toward the wall, toilet at my side, kids asleep, husband standing by. Just crying.

Take the Gifts
People Have to Give

You're probably good at giving. Many of us are, because we've been brought up to please people. There are times, however, when you have to stop giving and figure out how to take. It's not easy—but the rewards are huge.

People believe that food cures. Couscous and asparagus, baked chicken, turkey soup, macaroni and cheese, chocolate pudding, corn bread, broiled salmon, lasagne, tacos, strawberry smoothies. All these foods arrived on my doorstep, unbidden, like manna from heaven, during the time I needed wound care. They came from women in the neighborhood and women at church, from mothers of Carlyn's classmates and the director of Emily's preschool.

They came in Tupperware containers, Pyrex baking dishes, aluminum throwaway trays with green Saran Wrap stretched over the top. Sometimes they came four at a time, food piling up as though we were getting ready for a party or an earthquake. Each night, Rob and the girls and I would sit down to complete, hot, precooked meals, and though we had to constantly explain to the kids why the meatballs weren't crispy like mine or why the enchiladas didn't have extra cheese the way they like them or why we were having lasagne again when we knew they didn't like lasagne, we could go through the motions of normal life.

Taking a meal to someone is such a primal act. Even in our microwavable take-out, drive-through world, it survives like a flower pushing through the cracks in the cement. People can't do anything to help the fact that you have cancer in your breast or a wound across your abdomen, but they can drive you to the hospital every morning if you can't drive yourself, and they can do something about the fact that you will be hungry at the end of the day—and they do.

At first I cringed at so much goodwill. I knew that one of the mothers who brought me meals each Tuesday had a child with a broken arm. Another had a child who had recently been diagnosed as autistic. Still another had one child and was unable to have another. And they were bringing *me* spiced ham? I felt as if goodwill were a bank account that I was depleting, casserole by casserole. I agonized about how I would ever pay it all back.

It was Cassi, a twelve-year-old girl who is the eldest

child in a family with five children, a soccer player, a thank-you-card writer, a novel reader, and a cookie baker, who showed me that payment wasn't the point.

Cassi didn't believe much in the curative power of food. She put her faith instead in baby-sitting. She stayed with Carlyn and Emily while Rob and I went to our Wellness Community support groups every Tuesday night for twelve weeks. She would fold the doll clothes and put the picture books on the bookshelf and help Carlyn study for her spelling tests—and she wouldn't let us pay her a dime. I tried to be coy and shove the money in her jeans pocket but she shook her head and said, "No thank you. I don't want to be paid."

I took my case to her mother—thinking I was doing a good deed for a kid who wouldn't stand up for herself. Her mother said, "That's what we've counseled her to say," and I rearranged my thoughts to see that Cassi was only doing what her parents thought was proper.

"But that's not fair to Cassi," I argued. "She's giving us a ton of time."

"It was her idea," her father explained, changing the picture in my mind yet again.

"She's been looking for a service project she could really do herself, with her own talents, and you're it. We're going to continue to instruct her to refuse your money because we want to support her effort."

I glanced at Cassi, who was twisting her hair in the doorway. I thought, I'm a service project? I'm in bad enough shape to be a service project?

"Think how few chances a twelve-year-old has to serve," Cassi's mom explained, but instead of thinking of a twelve-year-old's reality, what I thought of was Lisa and how much I wanted to take enchiladas over to her house and how much I wanted to take her boys to the park and how I hadn't been able to do those things for her. I also thought of Bridget and how she had thanked me for letting her come and I thought of my sister and how she had kept calling to make sure I would still need help the week after Christmas, because that was the week she was able to come. We all want to feel needed. We all want to feel that we have something to offer. And what I had to offer, while I was sick, was an unconditional acceptance of the help people wanted to give.

I promised Cassi I wouldn't pay her until I felt well again, and I didn't pay her a nickel until late in February, when instead of a doctor's appointment or a cancer support group, Rob and I went out for dinner.

Lesson #11

Modesty Is Irrelevant

A body that's been treated for breast cancer may not be a pretty sight, but it can be an inspiring and moving sight, and it can be a sight that helps saves lives. Don't hide it.

From the moment the reconstructive surgery on my right breast was complete, I had an overwhelming desire to take my clothes off in public. I had to stop myself from unbuttoning my shirt in the middle of conversations or unbuckling my jeans in the middle of the front yard. I had to remind myself that in polite society, baring your body simply isn't done, even if your body bears your biggest news. Other people have a new job to tell about, a new house, a new car. I have a new breast, and because it's a breast made up of part of my old tummy, I have a flat new tummy as well.

It's not as if I ever had this desire before. I was never an exhibitionist. I was a bra-wearing, one-piece-bathing-suit-buying, midriff-covering kind of gal. Sure, I breast-fed my children on the park bench and the back booth of a few restaurants, but always under a blanket, with friends or family standing watch. And, yes, I sometimes opted for the large public dressing room over the private room with a wait, but I always turned toward the wall when I pulled my top off. I was comfortable with my body but modest. What happened after my surgery was that modesty became irrelevant and comfort won out, like an understudy who gets a chance at the leading role and refuses to give it up.

I was recently asked to sit for a seasoned cameraman who needed to take my picture to go along with a newspaper article I wrote about my breast cancer experience. He was an attractive middle-aged man, efficiently and expertly arranging me and my husband and my kids in various poses around our house and our yard to show that we were a happy family who had survived. My urge to take off my clothes was never stronger. I knew that anyone reading the story would be looking at my breasts. My smile, the set of my jaw, my eyes, and my family who surrounded me were only part of the story. The heart of the matter was my breast—so why not show it?

The first person I can remember showing was my minister, Ginna. She'd come to the hospital to see how I was doing. "Did you see my new breast?" I blurted, opening my hospital gown. I must have been showing people all along—Rob, my mother, Lori, Bridget—but I don't recall having done it. I remember asking Ginna because of what she said in response.

"I saw it, Jennie," she said. "But have you?"

I hadn't. I was terrified at what I might see and how I might feel. I was using other people's reactions to prepare myself for my first glimpse. They were the mirror I held up to learn about my new body, and what I learned from their reactions—their "Wow, it looks so real" and their "You can hardly even tell"—was that I wasn't going to be disappointed.

I finally looked one afternoon when Dr. Black came in with his Doppler machine to listen to the blood flow. I watched as he spread gel on a marker stitch and held the cool metal to my senseless breast. I watched, because it was a medical act, a technical act, and that gave me enough of a margin to be detached about what I might see. I watched, and I felt an instant affinity for what was there. It was, for all its red-lined angriness, still my body. It was, in all its strangeness, a beautiful shape. I felt as proud as a new mom.

It's a nippleless breast—a mound of tummy tissue with a three-inch patch of tummy skin where the nipple used to be. The surgeons saved the skin of my breast, but the nipple is breast tissue; it had to go. There are tiny tummy hairs on the patch of tummy skin, growing the wrong way, like blades of grass reaching for the sun. There's a thick red scar holding the patch on, and another one that goes back up under my armpit, but these are nothing next to the big scar on my abdomen. Technically, they call this the harvest site. I imagine that's what they say when they clear-cut a forest as well: it's just harvesting. The big scar starts at one hip, dips down like a grin, and meanders back up to the other hip. It's twelve inches long. At the center of the grin is a large, flat, shiny patch where the big wound was. It's tight as a drum. There's a little scar encircling my new belly button—holding it in, defining a new knot in a new and unnatural spot. I think it's too high. My old belly button had to go because we needed to use the fat underneath it.

∽

I let everyone else see it—the friends who come to my house—not only because I like to keep hearing the "Wow"s and "Amazing"s—but because I want them all to know that I'm not the same. I've changed. If I didn't take my clothes off, it's possible that you would never know. Even in a bathing suit, you'd really have to be looking to tell. I'm a miracle of modern cancer diagnostic technology and the recipient of a skin-saving mastectomy utilizing state-of-the-art microsurgery, and no one can tell unless I show them.

So I show, in the privacy of my own home, where it's allowed. I unbutton my shirt, pull aside my bra on the right side, and I show. I also show in the locker room at the gym, where there are elaborate, agreed-on codes about nakedness. I make a point of not making a point to cover myself with a towel. I walk—openly and wildly conscious—from the locker to the shower. And no one says a thing.

Rob has taken my cue about comfort. Whereas he used to be skittish about my impromptu striptease—laughing nervously and joking about his modest wife—now he likes to stay around for the show and add his narration about how long the surgery was, how advanced the procedure, how permanent the result. He also simply likes the new breast. It makes no difference to him that it's crisscrossed with scars, that it's numb and unfeeling, that it's a rearranged piece of tummy flesh. "There's just something about the shape of a breast," he says, shrugging his shoulders and attempting to explain the unexplainable.

The girls have their own ideas. They see my breast, too—when I walk to the shower or get dressed—and I don't try to hide it. Their risk of getting breast cancer is far higher than normal now, since they have a mother who was diagnosed before menopause. They will have to be vigilant about checking their breasts, testing their breasts, and listening for the voice that tells them something might be wrong. If they grow up seeing my scars and sensing my comfort with my new body, perhaps they will not grow up in ignorance and fear. Perhaps they'll simply believe that the body is mutable. It can be scarred, it can change, but it can still be beautiful.

"It looks like a pirate's eye patch," Carlyn said the first time she saw the breast. The second time she saw it, she said, "It looks like a lasso." She noticed the scar under the arm that time. When she got a glimpse of the big abdominal scar, she changed her mind yet again. "It looks like a giant smiley face!" she shouted. "With one eye winking." Emily asks if the scars are going to be there for very much longer, and when I say that they'll be there forever she can't quite seem to grasp that. She has an image in her mind of what the body looks like, and mine simply no longer fits it.

✎

A month after my surgery, I had my weekly checkup with Dr. Black. He prescribed a stronger antibiotic to fight the start of an infection in my wound, and sent me home. I was on my way out of the door of his office, when he came running after me. "Would you mind showing someone?" he asked. "A new mastectomy patient?"

I'd never shown a stranger. I hesitated about a second—then thought of Lori Molina and the night I went to her apartment to see her breast and how that had convinced me to do the surgery. I went immediately into the exam room and shook hands with the patient in the chair. She was twenty years older than I was. She was ashen. She held herself around her waist with her arms, protecting her breasts, thinking she might still have a chance to hold on to them. I smiled and saw that there was a point to all this—to my being there that day, at that moment. The woman was terrified, just as I'd been terrified. And now, only a month later, I was in a position to lessen her fears. I whipped my shirt off.

"I love my breast," I gushed, "and I don't even have a nipple yet. The stomach's not too bad," I lied. I could see her peering at me, and at the doctor who was tracing the scars and pointing out the softness of the tissue, explaining the advantages of the magic that he can do. I could see her softening, considering. Maybe this surgery would work for her. Maybe this surgery would make her feel whole again. Maybe my body is the best advertisement yet for getting an annual mammogram. I have scars, after all, but at least I'm here for show-and-tell.

Lesson #12

Sometimes the Good Die Young

O ne day, six weeks after my surgery and toward the time when my wound began to close over with a thin and shiny layer of skin, the mailman set a package on my front step. It was from Lisa. Inside was a CD of folk music from around the world, called *Women of Spirit*. The words on the jewel case were an excerpt from Maya Angelou's essay "In All Ways a Woman":

> *Being a woman is hard work. Not without joy and even ecstasy, but still relentless, unending work. Becoming an old female may require only being born with certain genitalia, inheriting long-living genes and the fortune not to be run over by an out-of-control truck, but to become and remain a woman commands the existence*

and employment of genius. The woman who survives intact and happy must be at once tender and tough. She must have convinced herself, or be in the unending process of convincing herself, that she, her values, and her choices are important.

There was a card in the package as well. On the front was a detail from a painting of a Madonna and child bathed in a golden light. The infant rested its hand and head on his mother's shoulder as he slept. The mother looked down and away, as if something caught her attention, but she wasn't going to move. There was a small smile on her lips and a sense of utter peacefulness about her face. Inside the card was a note:

Jennie,

I'm glad you're recovering from the surgery. I'm sorry I've been out of touch. I've had one complication after another—infections with the radiation, worrisome headaches (I'm having an MRI to be on the safe side), and I struggle to maintain a balance between being optimistic and realistic. Optimism can be a little taxing depending on what else is happening.

Fortunately, Nathan and the little boys are doing well. Nathan's taking two weeks off from work, so we've been doing little projects around the house. It reminds me of the time right before we got married.

I'd love to talk with you, Jennie. I keep thinking I'm rounding some kind of bend and then, shazam,

something else. That's been the hardest part of this
for me—not knowing what my body is going to do.
When will you be in SB next? Do you have to have
radiation? Stay strong, Jennie. Know that you are so
so loved.

> *Love, Lisa*

P.S. Happy New Year to your family from ours.

P.P.S. Last week before I sent this off, I got more
distressing news. The tumors have spread to my brain.
I am praying feverishly. . . .

I called her and listened to her describe her legs as
numb, her throat as raw, and her body as emaciated. She
spoke in a voice that sounded exactly the way it always
had—so full of energy, so quick to laugh. She told me
that Nathan was feeding her through tubes, and thinking
of Rob cleaning the wound I couldn't bear to look at, I
said something about how brave she was to let Nathan
into her illness like that. She said something lovely about
how it was a different kind of intimacy and how lucky we
were to have chosen the men we did. She said she had to
hang up to go help Nathan finish the dishes.

⌘

She died a week later, from pneumonia. She refused
antibiotics and she refused to be taken to the ICU for

heroic measures. She knew her last hours were her last, and she used them to say good-bye to the people she loved. I'm told that she said to her little sister she was sorry she had to leave.

Lesson #13

Make the Experience Matter

*Cure isn't a word the oncologists use for breast can-
cer. They use, instead, survival rates—how many
women live for how many years after they have had
cancer. So instead of saying, "I'm cured," you call
yourself a survivor, and then you learn that surviving isn't very different from what you were doing
before.*

Lisa never got to finish Annie Dillard's *Pilgrim at Tinker Creek,* and she never got to finish the mosaic wall she
was building in her garden. She didn't get to finish rais-
ing her two boys or loving her husband or applauding her
mother's efforts in Washington. I, on the other hand, am
still here to walk my girls to school, to make my husband
dinner, to write the story Lisa would have agreed was so
important to tell. I was even able to get on a plane and

go to Berkeley for Lisa's memorial service. I felt the damp chill of the rain outside the church. I saw the bright faces of the sunflowers on the altar. I heard the bold, brave words of the love poem that Nathan stood up and read. I climbed the stairs to Lisa's bedroom and saw the view of the bay she saw as she lay there dying—and I cried. I felt, I saw, I heard, I climbed, I cried: I'm still here.

The thing I'm most afraid of is not having the experience matter—of sinking back into my everyday life. Life so quickly returns to normal.

Sometimes people will still call me and ask how I'm feeling and I can hear the edge in their voice—the darkness that tells me they're not just talking about how my day's going. Sometimes there will be a moment when I can't remember what's supposed to be wrong and I'll think, What are they referring to? Do they know that my feet sometimes hurt after I play too much tennis? Do they know I've had bad allergies this year? Then I'll suddenly remember, Oh, right. I'm a cancer survivor now.

I can't exactly say that people are disappointed to hear that things are going well with me, but there's no drama in it and there's a certain letdown. It was the same thing with escaping chemo. The horrors of chemo are so closely associated with the horror of cancer that whenever I told people I didn't have to have chemo, I felt as if I was somehow cheating. There's no emotional intensity in saying "I'm *fine*." There's no neat and tidy ending to a cancer story where the protagonist doesn't die.

Six months after my mastectomy, I was in a dressing

room at a department store. My friend Sally was in the dressing room next to me. Carlyn and Emily and Sally's four-year-old daughter, Caylie, were crawling back and forth between our rooms under the partition that divided us. They were giggling and laughing and telling us how *fabulous* we looked in the dresses we were trying on. At one point, all the girls were on my side of the partition when I was standing in my bra and undies. My kids didn't even stop for a millisecond, but Caylie stood frozen in place and stared.

"What's that?" she asked, pointing to my stomach.

"Just a scar," I said, pulling on a shirt.

"What happened to you?" Caylie pressed.

"I had a big owee," I said.

Caylie accepted this answer, but I later felt as if I'd cheated her. I should have said the words *breast cancer.* I should have said the word *survivor.* I should have told her that I was fine now. I had something important to say to her about cancer, and I'd brushed off the chance to tell it.

It was because of this tendency to ignore what happened—to so quickly forget the days in the hospital and the nights on the bathroom floor, to so easily let go of the lessons I learned from cancer—that I signed up to walk in one of the big breast cancer fund-raisers. It's the kind of thing I hate—snarled traffic, endless parking nightmares, pit potties, the whole bustle and smell of thousands of bodies. I went, though, because I wanted to call myself a survivor.

⚮

I went, first, to the Survivors Booth, where I was given a white hat that identified me as someone who'd fought cancer. I began to cry the moment I approached the tent. I felt so proud. Next I went to the check-in table, where there were blank placards and thick blue pens to write the names of the people you were walking in memory and support of. I know a lot of breast cancer patients and survivors now, but I put only one name on my placard: Lisa. The Pointer Sisters came out to sing "The Star-Spangled Banner"—and I cried again. It was those words about bombs bursting and the long night and seeing the symbol of hope still there at the end.

Within a few minutes, I was out on the street struggling to keep track of Carlyn and Emily in the huge sea of people and worrying about Rob and my mom, who had put aside their differences so they could both come walk with me. I was thirsty and I had to go to the bathroom. Emily decided that the first five or so feet she walked were about as much as she could handle, and begged to be carried. She also announced that she was ready to go home. There were lots of people in white survivor hats—young people and old people, bald people and people in wheelchairs—so that the hats started to look just like any other fashion accessory. Everyone had a name—or two or three or ten—written in thick blue pen on the placard on their back. I began to feel ever so slightly less special. I could have been in line for the Rocket Rods at Disneyland or at a Memorial Day Street Fair—anywhere with big crowds and a mutually understood purpose.

But I realized that this was the point. We survive, and we blend right back into the crowd, and we don't know from day to day whether we'll be alive tomorrow, but at least if we get out there and tell our stories and call ourselves survivors, we know that we're alive today.

Epilogue

About nine months after my mastectomy, Dr. Black twisted a bit of skin on the tummy patch of my new breast and made me a nipple. A few weeks after that he tattooed it a rosy brown. I didn't let Rob see the tattoo until the scabs were gone because I anticipated—correctly—what his reaction would be. My new breast was no longer a novelty; it looked like the real thing. When I showed Rob, his jaw literally dropped open in amazement. The breast looks so much like my original one that it's both miraculous and a little disappointing: some of the drama of what was done to me is diminished by its success. It would be possible to glance at my breast, in the right light, and overlook the scars.

"That's the goal," Dr. Black said. "The goal is for all this to become boring. Someday you're going to forget my name. You may even forget you ever had breast cancer."

He's right, of course—that I sometimes forget what I've been through. There are hours and days that go by when the thought of cancer doesn't enter my head. It's like driving those long, open highways through the deserts of the American West: you drive and you drive and you drive and all you see are the rocks and the sage-brush and the telephone poles and you listen to your music and you drink from your thermos and you think that there's nothing in the world besides your car and the rocks going by and then suddenly a road sign pops up and it reads, "Barstow: 235 miles," and you remember that the reason you're out there is to get somewhere.

The road signs for breast cancer are the headlines in the paper; the solicitations to give money to friends who are walking the walks or to organizations who are finding the cure; the news that someone else you know has been diagnosed; a funny twinge or a rough patch of skin on your neck or your back or your breast or your toe; your mammogram appointment that you try to pretend is no big deal because you know it's going to be clean, but which makes you work extra hard to tie up any loose ends, just in case your life is, once again, thrown into crisis.

It happens. It happened to Lori Molina, of the red pin curls, the big, beautiful breasts, and the generous heart. She found a second lump near her collarbone. A bone scan revealed tumors in her brain. Her doctors did every-thing they could, but she died from breast cancer at the age of thirty-one. I only met her twice—the time she showed me her new breast and one time when I ran into her in Dr. Black's office—but I was devastated by the news of her death. I vowed that, to keep her memory alive, I would do for other mastectomy patients what she did for me. I would counsel them and encourage them and let them see my breast and show them by my example that cancer can make you strong and courageous and peaceful and pleased. Dr. Black gives my number to his patients who are particularly terrified, and they come to my house—a procession of frightened cancer patients.

"Are you ever going to have breast cancer again?" Emily sometimes asks me after one of these women has left.

"No," I say—and then I add the words that are closer to the truth: "At least I hope not."

"Am I going to have breast cancer when I grow up?" she asks.

"No," I say—this time unequivocally, because I trust that we'll find a cure, that we'll find the cause, and that all the lessons we learned will come to make a difference—"You won't."

Acknowledgments

This book was magic from the start and some of that magic came in small, steady doses from people I talk to every day. I'd like to thank my husband, Rob Robertson, for sharing the darkness as well as the light; my compatriot, Jo Giese, for always answering the phone; my neighbor Denise Honaker for long walks and open ears; my friend Lori Logan for her kitchen table wisdom; and my family— Laura Nash Caldwell, Sandy Nash, Rod Nash, and Honeydew Nash Murray—for cheering me on one more time.

Some of the magic came in the form of powerful and generous reactions, both to the idea of this book and to the manuscript at various stages of completion. I'd like to thank Betsy Carter, Judy Davis, Lisa Owens, Congresswoman Lois Capps, Nathan Brostrom, Joe Molina, Janet Barker, Claire Noland, Stewart Burgess, and Barbara Abercrombie. Thanks also to Bruce Hazelton and Kelle Brown for making me look so good.

Thanks to my wise and wonderful agent, Betsy Amster, for catching the spirit of this story so early, and to the fabulous team at Scribner for all their time and talent. I'd like particularly to thank my first editor, Jane Rosenman, for her perseverance and her vision; my second editor, Beth Wareham, for stepping into the fray with grace, wisdom, and patience; Rica Allannic and Ethan Friedman, the most professional editorial assistants on the planet (and to Ethan for the best reaction to the title); Stephanie Lehrer for her well-organized and professional publicity campaign; and Sue Fleming and Roz Lippel for putting so many pieces together.

Special thanks to Dr. James Jens Black for work that could inspire monuments as well as books; Dr. Anna Mellor for her incredible intuition; the people of Christ Church, Redondo Beach for their support, their casseroles and their prayers; Bridget O'Brian and Janet Krolman for their visits; and to all my friends, family, and Seaside neighbors who rallied to help me heal and then rallied to help me get the word out.